JEAN-JACQUES ROUSSEAU

The First and Second Discourses

JEAN-JACQUES ROUSSEAU

THE FIRST
AND SECOND
DISCOURSES

EDITED,
WITH INTRODUCTION AND NOTES,
BY *Roger D. Masters,*
DARTMOUTH COLLEGE

TRANSLATED BY ROGER D.
AND JUDITH R. MASTERS

BEDFORD/ST.MARTIN'S
BOSTON ♦ NEW YORK

Contents

INTRODUCTION   1

NOTE ON THE TRANSLATION   27

Discourse on the Sciences and Arts (First Discourse)   31

     EDITOR'S NOTES   65

*Discourse on the Origin and Foundations of Inequality
(Second Discourse)*   77

     ROUSSEAU'S NOTES   182

     EDITOR'S NOTES   229

Introduction

In the two hundred years since the publication of the *Social Contract* and the *Émile* in 1762, Jean-Jacques Rousseau has been condemned and praised, studied seriously and dismissed as eccentric. Acclaimed as a literary giant for the beauty of his *Confessions* or his *Reveries*, he has been damned as a "romantic"; considered one of the most important philosophers of the eighteenth century, his doctrines have been described as "necessarily inconsistent with each other"; praised as the clearest apostle of popular democracy, his political thought has been attacked as "totalitarian."[1] On every point, there is paradox.

Whatever the judgment, most of those who have debated the meaning, character, and value of Rousseau's work have admitted its historical and current importance. Not only have the politics and philosophy of Western civilization been, in the past, greatly influenced by Rousseau's thought; even today Rousseau is, with the possible exception of Voltaire, the most frequently cited and read author of eighteenth century France. Save the

---

[1] It is not possible to review completely the vast secondary literature on Rousseau. For bibliographical surveys, see Peter Gay's Introduction to Ernst Cassirer, *The Question of Jean-Jacques Rousseau* (New York: Columbia University Press, 1954), pp. 3-30, and Alfred Cobban, *Rousseau and the Modern State* (London: George Allen and Unwin, 1934), chapter ii. Many of the more useful secondary works are cited in the footnotes to this introduction.

1

specialist, how many of us have studied the works of Rousseau's contemporaries, Grimm, Helvétius, d'Alembert, Condillac, or even Diderot? The continued vitality of Rousseau's writings suggests that, in addition to their historic importance, they may have an intrinsic philosophic value that justifies our reading his *First* and *Second Discourses.*

Rousseau was born in Geneva in 1712, and after an errant youth he settled in Paris.[2] His major philosophic works were written in France, from which he fled in 1762 after the condemnation of the *Émile* by the Parlement of Paris. Following years of persecution and flight, made more bitter by Rousseau's belief that a conspiracy had been formed against him, he returned to Paris in 1770. He died on July 2, 1778 at Ermenonville. Despite his long residence in various parts of France, Rousseau was greatly influenced by his native city, and signed many of his works as a "Citizen of Geneva."[3]

A brief mention of the eighteenth-century setting is in order before we examine Rousseau's *Discourses.* In politics, this was the century of "enlightened despotism," symbolized by Frederick the Great of Prussia. The powers of traditional rulers, essentially unlimited by constitutional restraints, were often used arbitrarily. The French monarchy maintained its accustomed procedures, incapable of fundamental reform because of its unwillingness to challenge the vested rights of the

---

[2] See Editorial Notes 6 and 7 to the *Second Discourse.*

[3] The indispensable biographical source is still Rousseau's own *Confessions.* See also the three-volume study by Jean Guéhenno, *Jean-Jacques* (the first two volumes published in Paris by Grasset, 1948 and 1950; the third by Gallimard in 1952).

aristocracy. Unmindful of the revolt that was to usher in an Age of Democratic Revolution at the end of the century, European rulers fought a series of limited wars, which only further obscured the coming internal upheavals. One can almost speak of a calm before the storm: "*Après moi, le déluge.*"

In intellectual circles, however, calm was hardly in evidence. To understand the ferment of thought in eighteenth-century France, it is necessary to distinguish three main factors that form the philosophic background of Rousseau's work. The first of these was the "Great Tradition" of Western thought—what might be called the doctrine of the "establishment"—derived from the medieval inheritance of which St. Thomas Aquinas was the greatest representative. The orthodox segments of French society—church, king, and nobility—continued to insist on the unquestioned truth of Christian dogma, on the necessary and divinely sanctioned character of monarchy, and on the inherently rational character of the natural law that defined man's secular, moral, and social duties.

By the eighteenth century, however, these orthodox beliefs had begun to decay into mere ritual for many. In the preceding century, a powerful challenge to the traditional synthesis of reason and faith had already emerged. The naturalistic and secular philosophies of Hobbes, Spinoza, and Locke can be called the second major factor in the intellectual background of Rousseau's thought.

These seventeenth-century thinkers had, broadly speaking, questioned the rational basis of the established notions of natural law, political justice, and religion. Their religious beliefs were unorthodox:

Atheism, Deism, or Socinianism. They insisted that social and political justice needs a more solid basis than human reason, which is too easily led astray by prejudice, custom, and error. The alternative was found in nature, both in the sense of physical nature as the source of all ideas (Hobbes's materialism and Locke's epistemology), and in the sense of an individualistic, pre-social status as the reference point for natural law (hence the importance of the "state of nature" for Hobbes, Spinoza, and Locke). By adopting such radical bases for their philosophical speculations, the seventeenth-century philosophers hoped to avoid the uncertainties of traditional metaphysical disputes. Patterning their thought on natural science (or "natural philosophy," as it was called in the age of Newton), they aspired to a new kind of certainty, free from the errors of the orthodox teachings.

This profound criticism of the Great Tradition did not go unnoticed in the eighteenth century. On the contrary, there arose a movement dedicated to the diffusion of the new, nontheological rationalism modeled on the study of natural phenomena. This movement is the third element in the intellectual background of Rousseau's work; usually called the Enlightenment, its chief proponents are often described as the *philosophes*. Optimistic and skeptical all at once, critical of the prejudices and narrow-mindedness of those established in power, the *philosophes* believed that the mass of men could be "enlightened" by the spread of education and sound reasoning (such as was to be made possible by the massive *Encyclopedia* edited by Diderot). Once the erroneous beliefs of the age had been swept away, a more rational, just, and happy society could be established. Progress on earth was possible.[4]

While societies continued to be ruled by those who dogmatically maintained the established traditions of religion, politics, and morality, these traditions were undermined by the skeptical criticism diffused by the *philosophes*. The "Age of Enlightened Despotism" contained an inherent contradiction, since the enlightenment tended to destroy the despotism of absolute monarchy. Rousseau's thought, to which we now turn, lays bare the root of this contradiction.

ROUSSEAU: CLASSIC OR MODERN?

Although Rousseau is perhaps the most famous thinker of the eighteenth century, the curious paradox of his fame cannot be overemphasized: in his first major work, Rousseau radically rejected the outlook of the age he is often taken to represent. The decisive characteristic of eighteenth-century thought was the growing belief in enlightenment and progress, symbolized by Diderot's *Encyclopedia*. And yet, at a time when he was Diderot's best friend, Rousseau wrote a blistering attack on the enlightenment in his *Discourse on the Sciences and Arts* (the *First Discourse*);[5] the spread of

---

[4] For a caricature of this view, see Carl Becker, *The Heavenly City of the Eighteenth Century Philosophers* (New Haven: Yale University Press, 1932). Becker was certainly right in showing that the *philosophes* really believed that a perfected society was possible on earth; he was wrong in describing this as a "medieval" cast of mind.

[5] This essay won the Prize of the Academy of Dijon in 1750, and was published late in that year. For the history of the work, see the Introduction in George R. Havens, ed., *Jean-Jacques Rousseau: Discours sur les Sciences et les Arts* (New

the arts and sciences, far from being a good thing as most supposed, was challenged by Rousseau as a corrupting influence on society.

Because he attacks the basic preconceptions of his contemporaries, the spirit behind Rousseau's thought must be questioned: was Rousseau inspired by a classical or by a modern conception of man, nature, and society? Since the *First Discourse* so explicitly rejects popular enlightenment as morally corrupting, it might be assumed that Rousseau depends solely on premodern traditions to prove that his own age—modernity—is in error. It will be seen, however, that Rousseau's *Second Discourse*⁶ is based upon the principles introduced by Hobbes and Locke, who may be considered among the founders of the modern philosophical perspective. One need only mention the reputation of Rousseau as a forerunner of modern democracy (as well as his asserted responsibility for modern totalitarianism) to indicate that it is by no means easy to specify the underlying character of Rousseau's philosophy.

This is not merely a pedantic question of classification. The presupposition that the spread of reason and science makes possible a perfected life on earth can properly be called modern: it is the underlying assumption which motivates the mass of men today. But this

York: Modern Language Association of America, 1946), pp. 1-88. This critical edition is hereafter cited as "Havens."

⁶ This work, whose full title is *Discourse on the Origin and Foundations of Inequality Among Men*, was written for another prize competition of the Academy of Dijon, and published in 1755. See C. E. Vaughan, ed., *The Political Writings of Rousseau* (2 vols.; Cambridge: University Press, 1915) I, 118-23. This edition is hereafter cited as "Vaughan."

typically modern belief in progress through science, adopted in Rousseau's time and held (albeit more critically) in our own, cannot be exempted from analysis; in an age in which science has produced the means of annihilating the human race, we dare not fail to reconsider the consequences of the development and spread of human knowledge. Since Rousseau's attack on the arts and sciences is the most famous—and perhaps the most profound—known to us, the *First Discourse* can provide a basis for considering the predicament of man in the twentieth century.

THE ATTACK ON THE ENLIGHTENMENT: THE FIRST DISCOURSE

The structure of the *First Discourse* is simple. If one disregards the brief Notice and Preface added for publication, the work consists of a short introductory passage and two main parts. The First Part is explicitly devoted to "historical inductions" intended to prove the proposition that "our souls have been corrupted in proportion to the advancement of our sciences and arts toward perfection."[7] Having asserted that the society of his time is morally depraved, Rousseau formulates the relationship between corruption and enlightenment as a phenomenon that "has been observed in all times and in all places."[8] He proceeds to give examples of what might be called a "law" of history, since it is as predictable as the tides: Ancient Egypt, Greece, Rome, and Constantinople, as well as modern China, have all been corrupted by the spread of knowledge, whereas

---

[7] *First Discourse*, p. 39 below. (All citations of the *Discourses* refer to the translations in this volume).

[8] *Ibid.*, p. 40.

the Persians, Scythians, Germans, early Romans, and Swiss were both virtuous and unenlightened; Sparta was moral and Athens corrupt. Admittedly, individuals may be both wise and virtuous, but the prime exemplar of such enlightened virtue, Socrates, was a bitter critic of the arts and sciences.[9] Fabricius, the early Roman hero, would have been horrified had he returned to see the corruption of Rome caused by literature and the arts.

In the Second Part of the *Discourse*, Rousseau turns to an analysis of the "sciences and arts in themselves"

---

[9] A passage from Plato's *Apology*—Socrates' defense before the Athenian jury—is cited by Rousseau to substantiate his argument, providing a striking example of his use of incorrect or incomplete quotations to make both an obvious point (namely that part of the original passage which he transcribes) and a more subtle one (which can only be understood by comparing the original to Rousseau's version). In the present example, Rousseau omits Socrates' reference to the ignorance of politicians, and substitutes *artists* for *artisans*, thereby redirecting the Socratic criticism to the particular targets central to his topic. Compare *Apology*, 22a-23b (the passage *critical* of artisans which Rousseau mistranslates) with the *First Discourse*, p. 62 (where Rousseau *praises* artisans). It might be asserted that Rousseau's mistranslation is accidental or at any rate unimportant, but the rearrangement of this quotation—like that of many others elsewhere in his works—follows a pattern which is too contrived to be a product of carelessness or chance. On the possibility of "disguising" the truth in philosophic writing, see *Rêveries*, Promenade iv, in *J. J. Rousseau: Oeuvres Complètes* (Paris: Gallimard [Bibliothèque de la Pléiade], 1959, I, 1025-32; and Leo Strauss, *Persecution and the Art of Writing* (Glencoe, Ill.: The Free Press, 1952), especially chapter i. For an admission that Rousseau did not reveal his thought completely in the *First Discourse*, see his *Confessions*, Book viii (Pléiade, I, 388).

to explain the apparent contradiction between virtue and enlightenment. Human knowledge, whether of astronomy, rhetoric, geometry, physics, or morals, depends decisively on the prior existence of "our vices": the sciences are inherently dangerous. Rousseau specifies these dangers in detail. First, error is a more likely consequence of speculation than truth, so that study is not likely to achieve its proclaimed aim of knowledge. Second, the pursuit of the arts and sciences is a waste of time for a citizen. The discoveries of truly great scientists, like Newton, Descartes, and Bacon, do not directly teach the citizen to be virtuous; a fortiori, there is even less value in the works of the "crowd of writers" who try to disseminate philosophy, and who serve only to destroy faith and virtue. Third, enlightenment always produces luxury, fatal both to sound morals and to political power. Rousseau lists a series of conquests of rich and enlightened nations by poorer and warlike peoples. He shows that luxury, by corrupting men, also corrupts taste; Rousseau contrasts the degradation of overly civilized men with the "simplicity of the earliest times." Fourth, the arts and sciences destroy the military virtues needed by any political community for its self-defense; Rousseau again adduces historical examples to buttress his assertion that modern soldiers, while brave, lack true force and strength. Finally, the spread of the arts, by forcing men to recognize and honor talent, produces rewards based on appearances rather than recompenses for actions. As a result, inequality among men develops on an artificial basis, unrelated to true virtue.

Rousseau then praises the Academies (like that of Dijon), declaring that their functions mitigate the dangers of the arts, letters, and sciences, and again attacks the "crowds" of authors who diffuse learning.[10] Those who cannot go *far* in the sciences should be artisans,[11] whereas those who can make truly great intellectual advances—the "preceptors of the human race"—need no teachers: the functions of the *philosophes* and Encyclopedists, who try to spread knowledge, are either unnecessary or pernicious. Rousseau concludes that the true philosophers such as Newton, Descartes, and Bacon should become advisers to kings; only when political power and scientific knowledge work in harmony can the arts and sciences be profitable. As for the common man, Rousseau concludes that he should avoid study and knowledge, devoting himself to the practice of his true duty:

> Let us leave to others the care of informing peoples of their duties, and limit ourselves to fulfilling well our own . . . O virtue! . . . is it not enough in order to learn your laws to commune with oneself and listen to the voice of one's conscience in the silence of the passions? That is true philosophy.[12]

It takes little reflection to see that the *First Discourse* can be criticized as being self-contradictory: Rousseau criticizes the arts and sciences, yet he writes an erudite discourse for an academy of arts and sciences. Rousseau himself saw this problem:

---

[10] This praise of the Academies, it should be noted, is almost certainly ironic: an academy like that of Dijon included precisely the kind of "indiscreet" "compilers of books" whom Rousseau attacks in the sequel.

[11] Here we see one reason why Rousseau substituted "artists" for "artisans" in his quotation from Plato's *Apology*. See above, note 9.

[12] *First Discourse*, p. 64.

How can one dare blame the sciences before one of Europe's most learned Societies, praise ignorance in a famous Academy, and reconcile contempt for study with respect for the truly learned? *I have seen these contradictions, and they have not rebuffed me.*[13]

Given this assertion, the superficial inconsistency of the *First Discourse* can hardly be the ground for rejecting Rousseau's position; rather one must look for an underlying principle that could explain the paradox.

The reconciliation of "these contradictions" cited by Rousseau can be found in the conception of knowledge developed in classical antiquity, most notably by Plato.[14] According to many ancient philosophers, there is a fundamental distinction between the opinions of most men and true knowledge, accessible only to a few. The opinions of a given society at a given time are held uncritically by the average citizen, but he who would devote his life to the pursuit of wisdom must be willing to question such commonly held beliefs. Philosophy presupposes doubt; by examining popular notions with an open mind, one can come to understand the universal truths behind them.

The character and bearing of this classical dichotomy of knowledge and opinion may be clearer if some of the main points of Plato's thought are indicated. According to the *Republic*, the best political order that could be wished for would be rule by a "philosopher-king." But for Plato this is a paradox: Socrates speaks

---

[13] *Ibid.*, p. 34 (italics added).

[14] For a fuller analysis of the reasoning outlined in the following discussion see Leo Strauss, "On the Intention of Rousseau," *Social Research*, XIV (December, 1947), 455-87; and *Natural Right and History* (Chicago: University of Chicago Press, 1953), chap. vi (A).

of his fear that the idea of a philosopher-king will be laughed at as ridiculous and impossible.[15] It is paradoxical to talk of a philosopher who is king because the philosopher is motivated by a disinterested search for truth, whereas the king is concerned with radically different matters, such as material welfare and power, about which he must be partisan. Indeed, to realize the best political regime, Plato asserts that philosophers would have to be *compelled* to rule.[16] True philosophy —the impartial quest for wisdom—is essentially opposed to politics.

The opposition between politics and philosophy, derived from the distinction between knowledge and opinion, has far-reaching implications. Philosophy is the highest human activity, but it is an activity open to few men. For the rest of mankind—the "ordinary men"— philosophy is dangerous because it depends on a doubting of common opinions (like the belief that the laws and customs of one's own country are always right and just). Politics and political virtue are the standard for most men; patriotism is a positive good because only within a particular, "historical" society can the average man have an idea of what is good or bad.

The stability and soundness of popular opinion require a small community, relatively independent of foreign pressures, and composed of patriotic citizens who prefer the public good to private gain. But political virtue is, by itself, insufficient; the best society must also permit (and, indeed, require) a few men to study philosophy. These few must be able to doubt without shaking the beliefs of the many. When a

[15] *Republic* V.472-473.
[16] *Ibid.*, V.519-520.

society of virtuous patriots tolerates the existence of philosophers and permits them to direct its political destinies, the goodness of the citizens can be combined with the superior knowledge of which some men are capable. Any other solution, which attempts to merge knowledge with popular opinion, will produce neither stability nor wisdom.[17]

This restatement of Plato's conception of philosophy and politics, however imperfect, should at least indicate the classical elements in Rousseau's thought. Rousseau always criticized the political trend toward large states based on commercial economies, clearly in evidence by the eighteenth century. In the name of "virtue" he consistently emphasized the superiority of the small city-state of classical antiquity, mirrored in his native city of Geneva. He argued that it is impossible for the citizens of a large society to know each other and to concern themselves with the common good; men devoted to private economic enterprises cannot place the public interest above their own selfish desires. The only truly sound political community must be based on patriotism and virtue, like Sparta and republican Rome.

Rousseau consequently preferred the political conceptions of the ancients to those of the moderns: "Ancient politicians incessantly talked about morals and virtue, those of our time talk only of business and money."[18] To achieve justice, one must go back

---

[17] For example, see *ibid.*, VI.495.

[18] *First Discourse*, p. 51. Among recent interpreters of Rousseau, Bertrand de Jouvenel has been perhaps the most insistent in emphasizing Rousseau's reliance upon the ancients. See "Rousseau the Pessimistic Evolutionist," *Yale French*

to the classical conception of a small political únit animated by patriotism. If political improvement is possible, it is not that reform, based on a diffusion of scientific knowledge, which the *philosophes* contemplated. Since popular enlightenment is intrinsically corrupting, the education of the mass of men should be oriented toward the strengthening of healthy opinions, virtue, and patriotism.

This does not mean that philosophy or science is, as such, "bad." The few men capable of a disinterested search for truth are "the preceptors of the human race"; they alone can "raise monuments to the glory of human intellect."[19] But the role of the philosopher is that of an adviser to the ruler, and not that of a popular educator. The *philosophes* failed to see that there is an insoluble contradiction between philosophy and politics, a contradiction that can be resolved (insofar as such a resolution is possible) only on the grounds of classical thought.

THE ATTACK ON THE GREAT TRADITION: THE SECOND DISCOURSE

Rousseau's preference for certain themes in classic philosophy was not, however, merely a restatement of traditional views. One completely misses the main thrust of his thought if the extent of his criticism of accepted "orthodox" views is not perceived. The boldness of Rousseau's attack on the ideas normally de-

Studies, XXVIII (Fall-Winter, 1961-62), 83-96; and "Essai sur la Politique de Rousseau," in Jean-Jacques Rousseau, *Du Contrat Social* (Genève: Les Éditions du Cheval Ailé, 1947), pp. 13-165.

[19] *First Discourse*, p. 63.

rived from classical authors is most clearly seen in his *Second Discourse*, "a work of the greatest importance," which was intentionally shocking to most eighteenth-century traditionalists.[20]

The *Discourse on the Origin and Foundations of Inequality Among Men* is divided into four main sections: the Dedication, the Preface, and the two Parts of the body of the *Discourse*. The Dedication, written after the work was completed, praises the city of Geneva as a virtuous republic that satisfies all the requirements of the community which Rousseau would have chosen for his native land. While this praise is couched in terms sufficiently extravagant to permit one to question its sincerity, there is no doubt that the Dedication implies that the best political system is that of a small city-state in which the body of patriotic citizens is sovereign.[21]

The short, important Preface insists that the fundamental problem of political philosophy lies in the nature of man and the status of natural law. Rousseau thereby broadens his topic from the origin of inequality *per se* to the underlying basis of all standards of right

---

[20] *Confessions*, Book viii (Pléiade, I, 388-89). When Rousseau submitted this *Discourse* to the prize competition of the Academy of Dijon, the judges refused to listen to the reading of the entire manuscript. See George Havens, "Hardiesse de Rousseau dans le *Discours sur l'inégalité*," *Europe* (November-December, 1961), pp. 149-58. Rousseau claimed that he had expected the rejection of his essay. *Confessions, loc. cit.*

[21] For Rousseau's views on Geneva, see his *Letter to d'Alembert*, translated by Allan Bloom under the title *Politics and the Arts* (Glencoe, Ill.: The Free Press, 1960); and the *Lettres Écrites de la Montagne*, in *Oeuvres Complètes* (13 vols.; Paris: Hachette, 1909-1912), III, 117-267.

and justice. Rousseau rejects previous notions of natural law on the grounds that philosophers have as yet failed to discover the true nature of man: "so long as we do not know natural man, we would try in vain to determine the law he has received" (i.e., the law of nature).[22] In particular, it appears that no attention need be paid to "the ancient philosophers, who seem to have tried their best to contradict each other on the most fundamental principles."[23]

Having thus questioned the validity of all traditionally accepted notions of natural law, Rousseau turns in the First Part to an examination of man in the true "state of nature," which existed prior to the formation of the first human societies. He argues that man, living according to purely natural impulsions outside of society, was essentially a stupid but peaceful animal. Hobbes was wrong in supposing a natural state of war among men. Rousseau's criticism of Hobbes is, however, built on Hobbesian assumptions; natural man is impelled by the principle of self-preservation, and is not guided by innate reason as was assumed by those who followed Aquinas and the Great Tradition.

Hobbes's error, according to Rousseau, was that he imputed to natural man a number of qualities—foresight, pride, and fear of violent death—which are the product of *society* and not of nature. Man in the state of nature was not a "wicked child," but a "good" animal who never harmed another unless his own preservation was at stake. Rousseau goes further, and suggests that Hobbes's basic natural principle of self-preservation was moderated by natural compassion,

---

[22] *Second Discourse*, p. 95.
[23] *Ibid.*, p. 94.

which is present in animals. From these two principles of natural man—self-preservation and compassion—Rousseau claims at the outset that he can establish all the principles of natural right, "without the necessity of introducing [the principle] of sociability" which was assumed in the philosophical tradition of Aristotle, Cicero, and Aquinas.[24] The classical thinkers of the West do not provide the basis for a true understanding of the law of nature.

In the Second Part of the *Discourse*, Rousseau traces the "hypothetical history" of the origin of political society and social inequality as it developed out of the egalitarian independence of the state of nature. Changes in the human species, which took an incredibly long time, eventually led to the building of huts, the establishment of the family, the development of language, crafts, and arts, the emergence of pride and deception, and the invention of metallurgy and agriculture; finally the development of social cooperation resulted in the need to divide land and differentiate the work of one man from that of another.

Inequalities (especially inequalities of possessions) were thus created among men who, in the pure state of nature, had been equal. As men learned to think and calculate, they became fully aware of these inequalities and opposed each other in violent competition for the material means of existence. Hobbes's "war of all against all" was the product of historical development, and not the true "state of nature"; but such a "war of all" did occur, and its effects led to the foundation of civil society.

In the "state of nature" (i.e., prior to the establish-

---

[24] *Ibid.*, p. 95.

ment of political society) each man was his own judge; there was no superior to enforce any "laws." When men found their very existence threatened by violence in the warlike "last stages of the state of nature," they were inevitably led to conclude a "social contract"; a political community was founded to judge conflicts between individuals, transforming mere possession into a lawful right to property, and making possible the enforcement of standards of law and order.

Rousseau merely sketches the fundamental character of the political order created by the social contract:

> The people having, on the subject of social relations, united all their wills into a single one, all the articles on which this will is explicit become so many fundamental laws obligating all members of the State without exception, and one of these laws regulates the choice and power of magistrates charged with watching over the execution of the others.[25]

Here we find the essence of the teaching of the *Social Contract*, though the "single will" is not yet described as the "general will" (as it is in Rousseau's most famous work). Despite claims by some that there is a basic difference between the *Social Contract* and the *Second Discourse*,[26] the two works can be shown to be thoroughly consistent.[27]

---

[25] *Ibid.*, p. 169.
[26] E.g., Vaughan, I, 80-81.
[27] Cf. Émile Durkheim, *Montesquieu and Rousseau* (Ann Arbor: University of Michigan Press, 1960), p. 135. On the relationship between Rousseau's doctrine of the "general will" and his thought as a whole, see Leo Strauss, *What is Political Philosophy?* (Glencoe, Ill.: The Free Press, 1959), pp. 50-53.

Rousseau does not stop to analyze the principles of legitimate government in detail, however; he is concerned with a longer historical perspective that includes the ultimate establishment of unjust, tyrannical rule— "the last stage of inequality."[28]

> If we follow the progress of inequality in these different revolutions, we shall find that the establishment of the law and of the right of property was the first stage; the institution of the magistracy [i.e., governments] the second; the third and last was the changing of legitimate power into arbitrary power.[29]

The history of society passes through a stage of legitimate government under law, to terminate in the most extreme and indefensible inequality possible, under which the powerful oppress the weak within political society. Such a situation, according to Rousseau, is no better than a "war of all against all"; an illegitimate and despotic government can be overthrown by violent means with complete justice. There is an absolute right to revolution.

The radical implications of Rousseau's *Second Discourse*, while not difficult to infer from this position, deserve emphasis. Unjust government, in which a ruler is not subordinate to popularly enacted law, is illegitimate as well as contrary to nature; since "it is manifestly against the law of nature . . . that a child command an old man,"[30] hereditary monarchy apparently has no rational sanction that justifies obedience. This does not mean that Rousseau himself preached the desirability

---

[28] *Second Discourse*, p. 177.
[29] *Ibid.*, p. 172.
[30] *Ibid.*, p. 181.

of revolution, but he does deprive most forms of government of their philosophic respectability.[31]

Criticism of the existing state of human society as morally corrupt has often been identified as the core of Rousseau's teaching.[32] Here it is important to indicate the extent of Rousseau's attack on the vices of society, for he by no means limits his criticism to the corruption particular to the eighteenth century. On the contrary, Rousseau raises the more fundamental question of whether or not society *itself*, as well as the institution of property on which it is based, is good for the human species. Man in the state of nature was not virtuous, since true virtue requires control over natural impulsions and therefore depends on thought and social experience. But, by nature, man is *good*— self-sufficient, compassionate to others when they do not threaten him, and incapable of pride, hatred, falsehood, and vice. Society, precisely because it develops man's faculties, corrupts him.

It was often said of the *Second Discourse* that it challenged civilized man to return to the forests to live as a beast; Voltaire called it Rousseau's "book against the human race." Rousseau rejected this criticism, and never failed to insist that his analysis was merely intended to provide a sound philosophic basis

---

[31] See *ibid.*, note (*i*), p. 202: ". . . they will scrupulously obey the laws, . . . but they will nonetheless scorn a constitution . . ." Cf. *Social Contract*, Book III, chap. xv.

[32] See Charles W. Hendel, *Jean-Jacques Rousseau: Moralist* (2 vols.; London: Oxford University Press, 1934); de Jouvenel, "Essai sur la politique de Rousseau," especially pp. 15-20, 116; and E. H. Wright, *The Meaning of Rousseau* (London: Oxford University Press, 1929).

for understanding man, nature, and society. Nonetheless, it should be evident that Rousseau radically rejects all accepted, traditional justifications for the existence of political society and natural law. The nature of man does not include an innate reason that leads him to understand and obey natural law (as the Christian tradition derived from Aristotle insisted); the natural man is an animal who follows natural impulses without thinking. Property, although indeed a basis of political society, is open to profound criticism as the cause of "crimes, wars, murders, miseries, and horrors."[33] Society itself is not a blessing for man, who is not a "political and social animal" by his very nature (as taught by Aquinas). For Rousseau, the Great Tradition was untenable as it stood.

ROUSSEAU'S CORRECTION OF THE CLASSICS ON THE BASIS OF THE MODERNS

It has been argued above that Rousseau's *First Discourse* can best be understood as a criticism of the modern conception of politics; only the classical philosophers, who distinguished between knowledge and opinion, were properly aware of the possibility of a truly virtuous political community. In contrast, the *Second Discourse* sharply undermines the notions—derived from the classics of Greek and medieval Christian philosophy—on which society and justice were traditionally based in the eighteenth century. How can these seemingly opposed viewpoints have been formulated by one man within the space of five years? More specifically, how can the humble virtue of the patriotic

---

[33] *Second Discourse*, p. 141.

citizen be preferred to the enlightenment of the *philosophe* when society itself—and therefore the very possibility of patriotism—is criticized as "unnatural" and corrupting?

Here it is only possible to sketch an answer. Rousseau attempted to preserve the great insights of Greek philosophy by placing them on the foundations of a modern tradition which, from its inception, had attempted to refute the classical outlook. That is, he tried to re-establish the conclusions of Plato on Hobbesian premises, even though the latter had been directed against classic (and hence Platonic) philosophy.[34] He did this by insisting on understanding the historical process by which political life came into existence. Rousseau defends the superiority of the classical notion of virtue while asserting that virtue is the product of a historical development of the human species away from a natural state of merely animal "goodness."

Society is not natural, and since true virtue presupposes society, virtue is not natural. Before rational standards of justice—what Aquinas called "natural law"—can come into being, men must leave the state of nature and *create* human society. The formation of political communities is thus prior to justice and to some extent independent of it; brute force, deceit, and violence may be the necessary means of establishing the just so-

---

[34] This incredibly difficult and perhaps impossible objective explains in part the immense confusion which has arisen concerning the meaning of Rousseau's thought. Cf. Eric Weil, "J. J. Rousseau et sa Politique," *Critique*, LVI (January, 1952), p. 11.

ciety.[35] But once formed, there is a necessary logic which underlies political society and permits the philosopher to distinguish between "legitimate power" and "arbitrary power" or tyranny. The *emergence* of society can thus only be understood on the basis of the assumptions of Hobbes and modern political thought; the *proper ordering* of an existing political society must take into consideration the principles of classical philosophy.

There are two kinds of natural law or natural right: one (that of Hobbes or Spinoza) is the law of physical nature, which operates whether or not human reason has discovered it; the other (that of Plato, Aristotle, or Aquinas) is the law of rational man, operating only *after* it has been discovered by reasoning men within society. The first kind of natural right precedes civil society, the second presupposes it as natural.[36] Although these two kinds of natural law had almost always been opposed to each other as mutually exclusive alternatives, Rousseau, with extraordinary audacity, tries to show that they are not necessarily inconsistent.

---

[35] *Second Discourse*, pp. 158-60. See also *Social Contract*, Book I, chap. iii; Book IV, chap. iv (first footnote); and the context of the epigraph from Virgil's *Aeneid*. The necessary role of force in the founding of political society may go far to explain the influence of Machiavelli on Rousseau; see *ibid.*, Book II, chap. vii; Book III, chap. vi; and *Économie Politique* (Vaughan, I, 244).

[36] Rousseau considered the following sentences as a possible opening for the *Social Contract*: "Let us begin by clarifying an ambiguity which is the source of many sophisms. There are two ways of considering natural right." Fragment (Vaughan, I, 332). See also the two kinds of natural law discussed in the Preface to the *Second Discourse*.

INTRODUCTION / 23

The attempt to re-establish the classical understanding of politics on a modern foundation entailed an important shift in emphasis that distinguishes Rousseau's thought from Plato's and Aristotle's. Whereas the great thinkers of Greek antiquity had stressed the importance of the *political order* within which man becomes virtuous, Rousseau's conception of the state of nature leads him to emphasize *freedom* as the criterion for judging human affairs. Thus, in the *Social Contract*, a political regime must preserve "civil liberty," the social substitute for the "natural liberty" abandoned when men left the state of nature.[37] This change from virtue to freedom as the primary concern of political thought explains why Rousseau, who perhaps understood the classic philosophers better than any of his contemporaries, has remained one of the most influential thinkers of modern times.

CONCLUSION: ROUSSEAU'S PARADOXES

This outline of Rousseau's *Discourses* indicates the complexity of his thought and justifies the attention paid to his work in the past two centuries. His writings are not only profound, they are paradoxical. His *First Discourse* is a learned essay on the danger of learned essays; his *Second Discourse* establishes the nature of man as the criterion for judging society, but reduces the natural man to an unthinking animal. The *First Discourse* can only be understood as a return to classical principles; the *Second Discourse* uses modern

---

[37] *Social Contract*, I, vi-viii. Only a modern author could have penned the resounding lines that open Book I, chapter i of this famous book: "Man is born free, and everywhere he is in chains."

principles to attack the tradition derived from the classics.

These paradoxes are, perhaps, reflections of Rousseau's contention that the political life of man poses a virtually insuperable difficulty: "The subjecting of man to law is a problem in politics which I liken to that of the squaring of the circle in geometry."[38] Politics means the rule of some men over others, and yet such rule is legitimate only if it is subordinate to impersonal laws enacted for the common good by the sovereign people. But in the last analysis men must interpret the laws, and all laws, no matter how well conceived, are open to abuse by men acting from selfish passion. This paradox of politics ultimately forces the philosopher to see the injustice and immorality of specific political actions and institutions. Thus the tension between philosophy and politics, which Plato had so clearly seen and the *philosophes* so hastily denied, lies at the root of Rousseau's thought.

A final word. Rousseau was, of course, aware of the paradoxical character of many of his writings. In the *Émile* he warned:

Common readers, pardon my paradoxes: they must be made when one thinks seriously; and, whatever you may say, I would rather be a man of paradoxes than a man of prejudices.[39]

---

[38]*Considerations on the Government of Poland*, chap. i, in Frederick Watkins, trans., *Rousseau: Political Writings* (London: Thomas Nelson, 1953), pp. 161-62. See also *Lettre à M. le Marquis de Mirabeau*, July 26, 1767 (Vaughan, II, 160).

[39] *Émile*, Book ii (Hachette, II, 60).

Elsewhere he mused, in a footnote to a difficult passage:

> I would wager that at this point a thousand people will again find a contradiction with the *Social Contract*. That proves that there are even more readers who ought to learn to read than authors who ought to learn to be consistent.[40]

Lest we be "common readers" who, in Rousseau's terms, "ought to learn to read," we must study his thoughts carefully and resist the temptation to accuse him of simple inconsistency. Without such effort, the failure to understand his philosophy will be our fault, not Rousseau's.

---

[40] *Jugement sur la Polysynodie* (Vaughan, I, 422).

Note on the Translation

This translation is an effort to provide an English version that corresponds word for word (as far as possible) with Rousseau's French text. While this goal may cause some awkwardness (especially in the overly rhetorical Dedicatory Epistle to the *Second Discourse*), it has the advantage of permitting the reader to come to his own conclusions with the smallest danger that the translation will have imposed a particular interpretation.

As a basic text for the *First Discourse*, the excellent critical edition of George R. Havens (*Jean-Jacques Rousseau: Discours sur les Sciences et les Arts* [New York: Modern Language Association of America, 1946]) was used; for the *Second Discourse*, we employed the text in C. E. Vaughan's edition of *The Political Writings of Rousseau* (2 vols.; Cambridge: University Press, 1915), I, 124-220.

We would like to thank the Beinecke Rare Book Library of Yale University for permission to consult the first editions of the *Discourses* and a manuscript translation of the *Second Discourse* written by John Farrington of Clapham, England, in 1756. Farrington's version, which is superior to the other translations we have found, suggested solutions to several difficult problems. We would also like to thank Richard P. Duval for assistance in translating Rousseau's Latin quotations.

We thank the following publishers for permission to reprint quotations from the works indicated:

Thomas Nelson (Frederick Watkins, trans., *Rousseau: Political Writings*); E. P. Dutton, Everyman's Library (Richard Crawley, trans., Thucydides' *The History of the Peloponnesian War*); Clarendon Press (J. B. Moyle, trans., *Institutes of Justinian;* Mandeville, *The Fable of the Bees;* Ernest Barker, trans., Aristotle's *Politics*); and Harvard University Press (A. D. Godley, trans., Herodotus' *Histories*).

[NOTE: Since the first printing of this translation, the third volume of the Pléiade edition of Rousseau's *Oeuvres Complètes, Du Contrat Social—Ecrits Politiques* (Paris: Gallimard, 1964), has appeared. The critical editions of the *First* and *Second Discourses*, as well as the other texts in the volume, will doubtless be the basis of future scholarship, and the editorial notes to the *Discourses* (pp. 1237–56 and 1285–377) add many worthwhile precisions to those in this volume.]

Satyr, you do not know it.
See the note, pp. 47-48.

DISCOURSE

Which Won the Prize
OF THE ACADEMY
OF DIJON
In the year 1750

On the Question proposed by that Academy:
*Has the restoration of the sciences & arts
tended to purify morals?*
BY A CITIZEN OF GENEVA

*Barbarus hic ego sum
quia non intelligor illis.*
OVID.[1]

GENEVA
BARILLOT & SON

---

[1] Numbered footnotes are those of the editor, and will be found on pp. 65-74. Rousseau's own notes to the *First Discourse* will be found together with the text, as in the original.

Foreword

WHAT IS CELEBRITY? Here is the unfortunate work to which I owe mine. Certainly this piece, which won me a prize and made me famous, is at best mediocre, and I dare add that it is one of the slightest of this whole collection.[2] What an abyss of miseries the author would have avoided if only this first written work had been received as it deserved to be! But a favor that was unjustified to begin with inevitably brought upon me, by degrees, a harsh penalty[3] that is even more unjustified.

Preface

HERE IS ONE of the greatest and noblest questions ever debated. This discourse is not concerned with those metaphysical subtleties that have prevailed in all parts of learning and from which the announcements of Academic competitions are not always exempt; rather, it is a matter of one of those truths that concern the happiness of mankind.

I foresee that I will not easily be forgiven for the side I have dared to take. Running counter to everything that men admire today, I can expect only universal blame; and the fact of having been honored by the approval of a few wise men does not allow me to count on the approval of the public. But then my mind is made up; I do not care to please either the witty or the fashionable. At all times there will be men destined to be subjugated by the opinions of their century, their country, their society. A man who plays the free thinker and philosopher today would, for the same reason, have been only a fanatic at the time of the League.[4] One must not write for such readers when one wants to live beyond one's century.

Another word and I am done. Little expecting the honor I received, I had, since submitting it, reworked and expanded this Discourse, to the point of making in a sense another work of it; today I consider myself obliged to restore it to the state in which it was honored. I have merely jotted down some notes and left two easily recognized additions of which the Academy might not have approved.[5] I thought that equity, respect, and gratitude required of me this notice.

Discourse

Decipimur specie recti.[6]

HAS THE RESTORATION of the sciences and arts tended to purify or corrupt morals?[7] That is the subject to be examined. Which side should I take in this question? The one, gentlemen, that suits an honorable man who knows nothing and yet does not think any the less of himself.

It will be difficult, I feel, to adapt what I have to say to the tribunal before which I appear. How can one dare blame the sciences before one of Europe's most learned Societies, praise ignorance in a famous Academy, and reconcile contempt for study with respect for the truly learned? I have seen these contradictions, and they have not rebuffed me. I am not abusing science, I told myself; I am defending virtue before virtuous men. Integrity is even dearer to good men than erudition to the scholarly. What then have I to fear? The enlightenment[8] of the assembly that listens to me? I admit such a fear; but it applies to the construction of the discourse and not to the sentiment of the orator. Equitable sovereigns have never hesitated to condemn themselves in doubtful disputes; and the position most advantageous for one with a just cause is to have to defend himself against an upright and enlightened opponent who is judge of his own case.[9]

This motive which encourages me is joined by another which determines me: having upheld, according to my natural intellect, the cause of truth, whatever

34

the outcome there is a prize which I cannot fail to receive; I will find it at the bottom of my heart.

FIRST PART

It is a grand and beautiful sight to see man emerge from obscurity somehow by his own efforts; dissipate, by the light of his reason, the darkness in which nature had enveloped him; rise above himself; soar intellectually into celestial regions; traverse with giant steps, like the sun, the vastness of the universe; and—what is even grander and more difficult—come back to himself to study man and know his nature, his duties, and his end. All of these marvels have been revived in recent generations.

Europe had sunk back into the barbarism of the first ages. The peoples of that part of the world which is today so enlightened lived, a few centuries ago, in a condition worse than ignorance. A nondescript scientific jargon, even more despicable than ignorance, had usurped the name of knowledge, and opposed an almost invincible obstacle to its return. A revolution was needed to bring men back to common sense; it finally came from the least expected quarter. The stupid Moslem, the eternal scourge of learning, brought about its rebirth among us. The fall of the throne of Constantine brought into Italy the debris of ancient Greece.[10] France in turn was enriched by these precious spoils. Soon the sciences followed letters; the art of writing was joined by the art of thinking—an order which seems strange but which is perhaps only too natural; and people began to feel the principal advantage of literary occupations, that of making men more sociable by in-

spiring in them the desire to please one another with
works worthy of their mutual approval.

The mind has its needs as does the body. The needs
of the body are the foundations of society, those of the
mind make it pleasant. While government and laws
provide for the safety and well-being of assembled
men, the sciences, letters, and arts, less despotic and
perhaps more powerful, spread garlands of flowers
over the iron chains with which men are burdened,
stifle in them the sense of that original liberty for
which they seemed to have been born, make them
love their slavery, and turn them into what is called
civilized peoples. Need raised thrones; the sciences and
arts have strengthened them. Earthly powers, love
talents and protect those who cultivate them.* Civilized peoples, cultivate talents: happy slaves, you owe to
them that delicate and refined taste on which you
pride yourselves; that softness of character and urbanity
of customs which make relations among you so amiable
and easy; in a word, the semblance of all the virtues
without the possession of any.

By this sort of civility, the more pleasant because
it is unpretentious, Athens and Rome once distinguished themselves in the much vaunted days of

---

*Princes always view with pleasure the spread, among their
subjects, of the taste for arts of amusement and superfluities
which do not result in the exportation of money. For, besides
fostering that spiritual pettiness so appropriate to servitude,
they very well know that all needs the populace creates for
itself are so many chains binding it. Alexander, desiring to
keep the Ichthyophagi dependent on him, forced them to give
up fishing and to eat foodstuffs common to other peoples;
but the American savages who go naked and live on the yield
of their hunting have never been subjugated. Indeed, what
yoke could be imposed on men who need nothing?

their magnificence and splendor. It is by such civility that our century and our nation will no doubt surpass all times and all peoples. A philosophic tone without pedantry; natural yet engaging manners, equally remote from Teutonic simplicity and Italian pantomime: these are the fruits of the taste acquired by good education and perfected in social intercourse.

How pleasant it would be to live among us if exterior appearance were always a reflection of the heart's disposition; if decency were virtue; if our maxims served as our rules; if true philosophy were inseparable from the title of philosopher! But so many qualities are too rarely combined, and virtue seldom walks in such great pomp. Richness of attire may announce a wealthy man, and elegance a man of taste; the healthy, robust man is known by other signs. It is in the rustic clothes of a farmer and not beneath the gilt of a courtier that strength and vigor of the body will be found. Ornamentation is no less foreign to virtue, which is the strength and vigor of the soul. The good man is an athlete who likes to compete in the nude. He disdains all those vile ornaments which would hamper the use of his strength, most of which were invented only to hide some deformity.

Before art had moulded our manners and taught our passions to speak an affected language, our customs were rustic but natural, and differences of conduct announced at first glance those of character. Human nature, basically, was no better, but men found their security in the ease of seeing through each other, and that advantage, which we no longer appreciate, spared them many vices.

Today, when subtler researches and a more refined taste have reduced the art of pleasing to set rules, a base and deceptive uniformity prevails in our customs, and all minds seem to have been cast in the same mould. Incessantly politeness requires, propriety demands; incessantly usage is followed, never one's own inclinations. One no longer dares to appear as he is; and in this perpetual constraint, the men who form this herd called society, placed in the same circumstances, will all do the same things unless stronger motives deter them. Therefore one will never know well those with whom he deals, for to know one's friend thoroughly, it would be necessary to wait for emergencies—that is, to wait until it is too late, as it is for these very emergencies that it would have been essential to know him.

What a procession of vices must accompany this uncertainty! No more sincere friendships; no more real esteem; no more well-based confidence. Suspicions, offenses, fears, coldness, reserve, hate, betrayal will hide constantly under that uniform and false veil of politeness, under that much vaunted urbanity which we owe to the enlightenment of our century. The name of the Master of the Universe will no longer be profaned by swearing, but it will be insulted by blasphemies without offending our scrupulous ears. Men will not boast of their own merit, but they will disparage that of others. An enemy will not be grossly insulted, but he will be cleverly slandered. National hatreds will die out, but so will love of country. For scorned ignorance, a dangerous Pyrrhonism will be substituted.[11] There will be some forbidden excesses, some dishonored vices, but others will be dignified with the name of virtues; one must either have them or affect them. Whoever wants to praise the sobriety of the wise men of our day may do so; as for me, I see in it only a refinement of intemperance as unworthy of my praise as their cunning simplicity.*

Such is the purity our morals have acquired. Thus have we become respectable men. It is for literature, the sciences, and the arts to claim their share of such a wholesome piece of work. I will add only one thought: an inhabitant of some faraway lands who wanted to form a notion of European morals on the basis of the state of the sciences among us, the perfection of our arts, the decency of our entertainments, the politeness of our manners, the affability of our speech, our perpetual demonstrations of goodwill, and that tumultuous competition of men of all ages and conditions who seem anxious to oblige one another from dawn to dark; that foreigner, I say, would guess our morals to be exactly the opposite of what they are.

When there is no effect, there is no cause to seek. But here the effect is certain, the depravity real, and our souls have been corrupted in proportion to the advancement of our sciences and arts toward perfection. Can it be said that this is a misfortune particular to our age? No, gentlemen; the evils caused by our vain curiosity are as old as the world. The daily ebb and flow of the ocean's waters have not been more steadily subject to the course of the star which gives us light during the night[13] than has the fate of morals and integrity been subject to the advancement of the sciences and arts. Virtue has fled as their light dawned on

---

*"I like," says Montaigne, "to argue and discuss, but only with a few men and for myself. For to serve as a spectacle to the great and to show off competitively one's wit and one's babble is, I find, a very inappropriate occupation for an honorable man." It is the occupation of all our wits, save one.[12]

our horizon, and the same phenomenon has been observed in all times and in all places.

Consider Egypt, that first school of the universe, that climate so fertile under a bronze sky, that famous country from which Sesostris departed long ago to conquer the world.[14] Egypt became the mother of philosophy and the fine arts, and soon after, she was conquered by Cambyses,[15] then by the Greeks, the Romans, the Arabs, and finally the Turks.

Consider Greece, formerly populated by heroes who twice conquered Asia, once at Troy and once in their homeland. Nascent learning had not yet brought corruption into the hearts of its inhabitants, but the progress of the arts, the dissolution of morals, and the yoke of the Macedonian[16] followed each other closely; and Greece, always learned, always voluptuous, and always enslaved, no longer experienced anything in her revolutions but a change of masters. All the eloquence of Demosthenes could never revive a body enervated by luxury and the arts.[17]

It is in the time of Ennius and Terence[18] that Rome, founded by a shepherd and made famous by farmers, begins to degenerate. But after Ovid, Catullus, Martial, and that crowd of obscene authors whose names alone alarm decency, Rome, formerly the temple of virtue, becomes the theatre of crime, the shame of nations, and the plaything of barbarians. That world capital finally falls under the yoke she had imposed on so many peoples, and the day of her fall was the eve of the day one of her citizens was given the title Arbiter of Good Taste.[19]

What shall I say about that capital of the Eastern Empire which, by its position, seemed destined to be the capital of the whole world, that refuge of the sciences and arts when they were banned from the rest of Europe perhaps more through wisdom than barbarism. All that is most shameful in debauchery and corruption, most heinous in betrayals, assassinations and poisons, most atrocious in the combination of all crimes, forms the fabric of the history of Constantinople. Such is the pure source from which we received the enlightenment of which our century boasts.

But why seek in remote times proofs of a truth for which we have existing evidence before our eyes. In Asia there is an immense country where honors for learning lead to the highest offices of the State. If the sciences purified morals, if they taught men to shed their blood for their country, if they aroused courage, the peoples of China would be wise, free, and invincible. But if there is no vice that does not dominate them, no crime with which they are not familiar; if neither the enlightenment of government officials, nor the supposed wisdom of laws, nor the multitude of inhabitants of that vast empire were able to save it from the yoke of the ignorant and coarse Tartar, what purpose did all its learned men serve? What benefit has resulted from the honors bestowed on them? Could it consist in being populated by slaves and wicked men?

Contrast these pictures with that of the morals of those few peoples who, preserved from this contamination of vain knowledge, have by their own virtues created their own happiness and an example for other nations. Such were the first Persians, an extraordinary nation where one learned virtue as one learns science among us, which conquered Asia with such ease, and which alone was honored by having the history of its institutions taken for a philosophic novel.[20] Such were the Scythians, about whom we have been left magnificent praises. Such were the Germans, whose simplicity, innocence, and virtues a writer—tired of tracing the crimes and foul deeds of an educated, opulent, and voluptuous people—took comfort in describing.²¹ Such had been Rome itself at the time of its poverty and ignorance. Such to this day, finally, is that rustic nation so much praised for its courage, which could not be destroyed by adversity, and for its fidelity, which could not be corrupted by bad example.*

It is not through stupidity that the latter have preferred other exercises to those of the mind. They were not unaware that in other lands idle men spent their lives debating about the greatest good, vice and virtue; and that proud reasoners, giving themselves the highest praises, lumped all other peoples together under the contemptuous name of barbarians. But they considered their morals and learned to disdain their doctrine.†

---

*I dare not speak of those happy nations which do not even know by name the vices we have so much trouble repressing, those savages in America whose simple and natural regulations Montaigne does not hesitate to prefer not only to the Laws of Plato, but even to everything philosophy could ever imagine as most perfect for the government of peoples. He cites numerous striking examples for anyone who would know how to appreciate them. But just think, he says, they don't wear pants!²²

† In good faith, will someone tell me what opinion the Athenians themselves must have had concerning eloquence when they so carefully kept it away from that upright tribunal against whose judgments the gods themselves never appealed? What did the Romans think of medicine when they banished it from their Republic? And when a remnant of humanity brought the Spanish to forbid their lawyers to enter America, what idea must they have had of jurisprudence? Could one

Could I forget that in the very heart of Greece rose that city as renowned for its happy ignorance as for the wisdom of its laws, that republic of demi-gods rather than men, so superior did their virtues seem to human nature? O Sparta! you eternally put to shame a vain doctrine! While the vices which accompany the fine arts entered Athens together with them, while a tyrant there so carefully collected the works of the prince of poets,[24] you chased the arts and artists, the sciences and scientists away from your walls.

That event was evidence of the following difference. Athens became the abode of civility and good taste, the country of orators and philosophers. The elegance of buildings there corresponded to that of the language. Marble and canvas, animated by the hands of the most skillful masters, were seen everywhere. From Athens came those astonishing works that will serve as models in all corrupt ages. The picture of Lacedaemon is less brilliant. "There," said other peoples, "men are born virtuous and the very air of the country seems to instill virtue." Of its inhabitants nothing is left to us except the memory of their heroic actions. Should such monuments be worth less to us than the curious statues Athens has left us?[25]

Some wise men, it is true, resisted the general torrent and kept themselves from vice while dwelling with the Muses. But listen to the judgment that the first and most unhappy of them made of the learned men and artists of his time.

"I examined the poets," he says, "and I consider them to be men whose talent deceives themselves and

---

not say that they believed they atoned, by this one act, for all the evils they had caused those unfortunate Indians.[23]

others, who claim to be wise men, who are taken to be such, and who are nothing of the kind.

"From poets," continues Socrates, "I turned to artists. No one knew less of the arts than I; no one was more convinced that artists possessed some very beautiful secrets. However, I perceived that their condition is no better than that of the poets, and that they are all under the same illusion. Because the most skillful among them excel in their specialty, they consider themselves the wisest of men. This presumption altogether tarnished their knowledge in my eyes. So it was that, putting myself in the place of the oracle and asking myself which I would rather be, what I am or what they are, to know what they have learned or to know that I know nothing, I answered myself and the god: I want to remain what I am.

"We do not know, neither the sophists, nor the poets, nor the orators, nor the artists, nor I, what is the true, the good, and the beautiful. But between us there is this difference: although those men know nothing, they all think they know something; whereas, if I know nothing, at least I am not in doubt of it. Hence all that superior wisdom attributed to me by the oracle reduces itself solely to my firm conviction that I am ignorant of what I do not know."[26]

There you have the wisest of men according to the judgment of the gods and the most learned Athenian according to the opinion of all Greece, Socrates, eulogizing ignorance. Can it be believed that if he were reborn among us, our learned men and artists would make him change his mind? No, gentlemen, this just man would continue to scorn our vain sciences; he would not help to enlarge that mass of books by which we are flooded from all sides; and, as he did before, he would leave behind to his disciples and our posterity no other moral precept than the example and memory of his virtue. Thus is it noble to teach men!

What Socrates had begun in Athens, Cato the Elder[27] continued in Rome, inveighing against those cunning and subtle Greeks who seduced the virtue and enervated the courage of his fellow citizens. But the sciences, arts, and dialectic again prevailed: Rome was filled with philosophers and orators; military discipline was neglected, agriculture was scorned, sects were embraced and the fatherland forgotten. The sacred names of liberty, disinterestedness, obedience to laws were replaced by the names of Epicurus, Zeno, Arcesilas.[28] "Since learned men have begun to appear among us," said their own philosophers, "good men have disappeared."[29] Until then, the Romans had been content to practice virtue; all was lost when they began to study it.

O Fabricius! What would your noble soul have thought if, restored to life to your own misfortune, you had seen the pompous appearance of that Rome saved by your valor and better glorified by your worthy name than by all its conquests? "Gods," you would have said, "what has become of those thatched roofs and those rustic hearths where moderation and virtue used to dwell?

"What disastrous splendor has succeeded Roman simplicity? What is this strange language? What are these effeminate customs? What is the meaning of these statues, these paintings, these buildings? Madmen, what have you done? Have you, the masters of nations, made yourselves slaves of the frivolous men you conquered? Are these rhetoricians who govern you? Is it to enrich architects, painters, sculptors, and comedians that you watered Greece and Asia with your blood? Are the spoils of Carthage the booty of a flute player? Romans, hasten to tear down these amphitheatres, break these marble statues, burn these paintings, chase out these slaves who subjugate you and whose fatal arts corrupt you. Let other hands win fame by vain talents; the only talent worthy of Rome is that of conquering the world and making virtue reign in it. When Cineas took our Senate for an assembly of kings,[30] he was dazzled neither by vain pomp nor by affected elegance. He did not hear that frivolous eloquence which is the study and charm of futile men. What then did Cineas see of such majesty? O citizens, he saw a sight that could never be produced by your wealth or all your arts, the most noble sight that has ever appeared beneath the heavens, the assembly of two hundred virtuous men, worthy of commanding Rome and governing the Earth."

But let us leap over the interval of space and time and see what has happened in our countries and under our own eyes; or rather, let us set aside odious pictures which would offend our delicacy, and spare ourselves the trouble of repeating the same things under different names. It was not in vain that I called up the shade of Fabricius; and what did I make that great man say that I might not have put into the mouth of Louis XII or Henry IV?[31] Among us, it is true, Socrates would not have drunk the hemlock; but he would have drunk from an even more bitter cup: insulting ridicule and scorn a hundred times worse than death.

Behold how luxury, licentiousness, and slavery have in all periods been punishment for the arrogant attempts we have made to emerge from the happy ignorance in which eternal wisdom had placed us. The heavy veil with which she covered all her operations seemed to warn us adequately that she did not destine us for vain studies. Is there even one of her lessons from which we have known how to profit, or which we have neglected with impunity? Peoples, know once and for all that nature wanted to keep you from being harmed by knowledge just as a mother wrests a dangerous weapon from her child's hands; that all the secrets she hides from you are so many evils from which she protects you, and that the difficulty you find in educating yourselves is not the least of her benefits. Men are perverse; they would be even worse if they had the misfortune to be born learned.

How humiliating for humanity are these reflections! How mortified our pride must be! What! could probity be the daughter of ignorance? Could knowledge and virtue be incompatible? What conclusions might not be drawn from these opinions? But to reconcile these apparent contradictions it is only necessary to examine closely the vanity and emptiness of those proud titles that dazzle us, and that we so freely give to human learning. Let us therefore consider the sciences and arts in themselves. Let us see what must result from their progress; and let us no longer hesitate to agree on all points where our reasoning will be found to coincide with historical inductions.

SECOND PART

It was an ancient tradition, passed from Egypt to Greece, that a god who was hostile to the tranquillity of mankind was the inventor of the sciences.*[32] What

---

*The allegory in the fable of Prometheus is easily seen; and it does not seem that the Greeks who riveted him on the Caucasus thought any more favorably of him than did the

must the Egyptians themselves, in whose country the sciences were born, have thought of them? They were able to see at first hand the sources that produced them. In fact, whether one leafs through the annals of the world or supplements uncertain chronicles with philosophic research, human learning will not be found to have an origin corresponding to the idea we like to have of it. Astronomy was born from superstition; eloquence from ambition, hate, flattery, and falsehood; geometry from avarice; physics from vain curiosity; all, even moral philosophy, from human pride. Thus the sciences and arts owe their birth to our vices; we would be less doubtful of their advantages if they owed it to our virtues.

The defect of their origin is recalled to us only too clearly in their objects. What would we do with arts without the luxury that nourishes them? Without the injustices of men, what purpose would jurisprudence serve? What would history become, if there were neither tyrants nor wars nor conspirators? In a word, who would want to spend his life in sterile speculations if each of us, consulting only the duties of man and the needs of nature, had time for nothing except his fatherland, the unfortunate, and his friends? Are we destined then to die fixed to the edge of the pit where the truth has hidden?[35] This reflection alone should rebuff, from the outset, any man who would seriously seek to educate himself by the study of philosophy.

Egyptians of their god Thoth. "The satyr," an ancient fable relates, "wanted to kiss and embrace fire the first time he saw it; but Prometheus cried out to him: Satyr, you will mourn the beard on your chin, for fire burns when one touches it."[33] This is the subject of the frontispiece.[34]

What dangers there are! What false paths when investigating the sciences! How many errors, a thousand times more dangerous than the truth is useful, must be surmounted in order to reach the truth? The disadvantage is evident, for falsity is susceptible of infinite combinations, whereas truth has only one form. Besides, who seeks it sincerely? Even with the best intentions, by what signs is one certain to recognize it? In this multitude of different opinions, what will be our *criterium* in order to judge it properly?* And hardest of all, if by luck we finally find it, who among us will know how to make good use of the truth?

If our sciences are vain in the objects they have in view, they are even more dangerous in the effects they produce. Born in idleness, they nourish it in turn; and irreparable loss of time is the first injury they necessarily cause society. In politics as in ethics, it is a great evil to fail to do good, and every useless citizen may be considered a pernicious man. Answer me then, illustrious philosophers—you who taught us in what proportions bodies attract each other in a vacuum; what are, in the orbits of planets, the ratios of areas covered in equal time intervals; what curves have conjugate points, points of inflexion, and cusps; how man sees everything in God; how soul and body could be in harmony, like two clocks, without communicating; which stars could be inhabited; what insects breed in an extraordinary

---

*The less one knows, the more he thinks he knows. Did the Peripatetics have doubts about anything? Did Descartes not construct the universe with cubes and vortices? And even today, is there in Europe any trivial physicist who does not boldly explain the profound mystery of electricity, which will perhaps be forever the despair of true philosophers?

manner[36]—answer me, I say, you from whom we have received so much sublime knowledge: had you taught us none of these things, would we consequently be fewer in number, less well governed, less formidable, less flourishing or more perverse? Reconsider, then, the importance of your products; and if the works of the most enlightened of our learned men and our best citizens provide us with so little that is useful, tell us what we must think of that crowd of obscure writers and idle men of letters who uselessly consume the substance of the State.

Did I say idle? Would God they really were! Morals would be healthier and society more peaceful. But these vain and futile declaimers go everywhere armed with their deadly paradoxes, undermining the foundations of faith, and annihilating virtue. They smile disdainfully at the old-fashioned words of fatherland and religion, and devote their talents and philosophy to destroying and debasing all that is sacred among men. Not that at bottom they hate either virtue or our dogmas; they are enemies of public opinion, and to bring them to the foot of altars it would suffice to send them among atheists. O passion to gain distinction, of what are you not capable?

The misuse of time is a great evil. Other evils that are even greater accompany letters and arts. Luxury, born like them from the idleness and vanity of men, is such an evil. Luxury rarely develops without the sciences and arts, and they never develop without it. I know that our philosophy, always rich in peculiar maxims, holds contrary to the experience of all centuries that luxury produces the splendor of States; but having forgotten the necessity for sumptuary laws, will our philosophy still dare deny that good morals are essential

to the stability of empires, and that luxury is diametric-
ally opposed to good morals? Granted that luxury is a
sure sign of wealth; that it even serves, if you like, to
increase wealth. What conclusion must be drawn from
this paradox so worthy of our time; and what will become of virtue when one must get rich at any price?
Ancient politicians incessantly talked about morals and
virtue, those of our time talk only of business and
money. One will tell you that in a given country a
man is worth the price he would fetch in Algiers; another, following this calculation, will discover some
countries where a man is worth nothing and others
where he is worth less than nothing.[37] They evaluate
men like herds of cattle. According to them a man is
worth no more to the State than the value of his domestic consumption. Thus one Sybarite would have
been worth at least thirty Lacedaemonians. Guess, then,
which of these two republics, Sparta or Sybaris, was subjugated by a handful of peasants and which made Asia
tremble.

The Monarchy of Cyrus was conquered with thirty
thousand men by a prince who was poorer than the least
significant Persian satrap; and the Scythians, the most
miserable of peoples, successfully resisted the world's
most powerful kings. Two famous republics competed
for World Empire: one of them was very rich, the other
had nothing, and it was the latter which destroyed the
former. The Roman Empire, in turn, after devouring all
the wealth of the universe, was the prey of people who
did not even know what wealth was. The Franks conquered the Gauls, and the Saxons England, with no
other treasures than their bravery and poverty. A group
of poor mountaineers, whose greed was limited to a

few sheepskins, after taming Austrian pride crushed
that opulent and formidable House of Burgundy which
made Europe's potentates tremble. Finally, all the
power and wisdom of the successor of Charles V, sup-
ported by all the treasures of the Indies, were shattered
by a handful of herring-fishers.[38] Let our politicians
deign to suspend their calculations in order to think
over these examples, and let them learn for once that
with money one has everything, except morals and
citizens.

Precisely what, then, is at issue in this question of
luxury? To know whether it is more important for
Empires to be brilliant and transitory or virtuous and
durable. I say brilliant, but with what luster? Ostenta-
tious taste is rarely combined in the same souls with the
taste for honesty. No, it is not possible that minds
degraded by a multitude of futile concerns could ever
rise to anything great, and even if they should have the
strength, the courage would be lacking.

Every artist wants to be applauded. The praises of
his contemporaries are the most precious part of his
reward. What will he do to obtain praise, therefore, if
he has the misfortune to be born among a people and
at a time when the learned, having themselves become
fashionable, have enabled frivolous youth to set the
tone; when men have sacrificed their taste to the tyrants
of their liberty;* when, because one of the sexes dares

---

*I am very far from thinking that this ascendancy of
women is in itself an evil. It is a gift given them by nature
for the happiness of the human race. Better directed, it could
produce as much good as today it does harm. We do not
adequately suspect the advantages that would result for society if a better education were given to that half of the
human race which governs the other. Men will always be
what is pleasing to women; therefore if you want them to be-

approve only what is suited to the weakness of the other, masterpieces of dramatic poetry are dropped and marvels of harmony rejected.[40] What will an artist do, gentlemen? He will lower his genius to the level of his time, and will prefer to compose ordinary works which are admired during his lifetime instead of marvels which would not be admired until long after his death. Tell us, famed Arouet,[41] how many vigorous and strong beauties have you sacrificed to our false delicacy, and how many great things has the spirit of gallantry, so fertile in small things, cost you?

Thus the dissolution of morals, a necessary consequence of luxury, leads in turn to the corruption of taste. And if, by chance, among the men distinguished by their talents, there is one who has firmness in his soul and refuses to yield to the spirit of his times and disgrace himself by childish works, woe to him. He will die in poverty and oblivion. Would that this were a prediction I make and not an experience I relate! Carle, Pierre,[42] the moment has come when that brush destined to increase the majesty of our temples with sublime and saintly paintings will fall from your hands, or will be prostituted to ornament carriage panels with lascivious paintings. And you, rival of Praxiteles and Phidias, you whose chisel the ancients would have commissioned to make gods capable of excusing their idolatry in our eyes; inimitable Pigalle,[43] your hand will be reduced to sculpting the belly of an ape or it must stay idle.

One cannot reflect on morals without delighting in

come great and virtuous, teach women what greatness of soul and virtue are. The reflections occasioned by this subject and made long ago by Plato greatly deserve to be better developed by a writer worthy of following such a master and defending so noble a cause.[89]

the recollection of the simplicity of the earliest times. It is a lovely shore, adorned by the hands of nature alone, toward which one incessantly turns one's eyes and from which one regretfully feels oneself moving away. When innocent and virtuous men enjoyed having gods as witnesses of their actions, they lived together in the same huts; but soon becoming evil, they tired of these inconvenient spectators and relegated them to magnificent temples. Finally, they chased the gods out in order to live in the temples themselves, or at least the temples of the gods were no longer distinguishable from the houses of the citizens. This was the height of depravity, and vices were never carried further than when they could be seen, so to speak, propped up on columns of marble, and engraved on corinthian capitals at the entry of great men's palaces.

While living conveniences multiply, arts are perfected and luxury spreads, true courage is enervated, military virtues disappear, and this too is the work of the sciences and of all those arts which are exercised in the shade of the study. When the Goths ravaged Greece, all the libraries were saved from burning only by the opinion, spread by one among them, that they should let the enemy keep belongings so well suited to turn them away from military exercise and amuse them with idle and sedentary occupations. Charles VIII found himself master of Tuscany and the Kingdom of Naples virtually without having drawn his sword; and his whole court attributed this unhoped for ease to the fact that the Princes and nobility of Italy enjoyed themselves becoming ingenious and learned more than they exerted themselves becoming vigorous and warlike. In fact, says the sensible man who relates these two anecdotes,[44] all examples teach us that in such military regulations, and in all regulations that resemble them, study of the sciences is much more apt to soften and enervate courage than to strengthen and animate it.

The Romans admitted that military virtue died out among them to the degree that they became connoisseurs of paintings, engravings, jeweled vessels, and began to cultivate the fine arts. And, as if that famous country were destined to serve unceasingly as an example to other peoples, the rise of the Medicis and the revival of letters brought about anew, and perhaps for always, the fall of that warlike reputation which Italy seemed to have recovered a few centuries ago.

The ancient Greek republics, with that wisdom which shone through most of their institutions, forbade their citizens the practice of those tranquil and sedentary occupations which, by weighing down and corrupting the body, soon enervate the vigor of the soul. What view of hunger, thirst, fatigues, dangers, and death can men have if they are crushed by the smallest need and rebuffed by the least difficulty? Where will soldiers find the courage to bear excessive work to which they are totally unaccustomed? With what kind of spirit will they make forced marches under officers who do not even have the strength to travel on horseback? Let no one raise as an objection the renowned valor of all those modern warriors who are so scientifically disciplined. I hear their bravery on a single day of battle highly praised, but I am not told how they bear overwork, how they endure the rigor of the seasons and the bad weather. Only a little sun or snow, or the lack of a few superfluities is necessary to dissolve and destroy the best of our armies in a few days. Intrepid warriors, ad-

mit for once the truth you so rarely hear: you are brave,
I know; you would have triumphed with Hannibal at
Cannae and at Trasimene; with you Caesar would have
crossed the Rubicon and enslaved his country; but it is
not with you that the former would have crossed the
Alps and the latter conquered your ancestors.

Fighting does not always win wars, and for generals
there is an art superior to that of winning battles. A
man who runs intrepidly into the line of fire is nonetheless a very bad officer. Even in the soldier, a little
more strength and vigor would perhaps be more necessary than such bravery, which does not preserve him
from death; and what does it matter to the State
whether its troops perish by fever and cold or by the
enemy's sword.

If cultivating the sciences is harmful to warlike qualities, it is even more so to moral qualities. From our
earliest years a foolish education adorns our mind and
corrupts our judgment. I see everywhere immense institutions where young people are brought up at great
expense, learning everything except their duties. Your
children will not know their own language, but they
will speak others that are nowhere in use; they will know
how to write verses they can barely understand; without
knowing how to distinguish error from truth, they will
possess the art of making them both unrecognizable to
others by specious arguments. But they will not know
what the words magnanimity, equity, temperance, humanity, courage are; that sweet name fatherland will
never strike their ear; and if they hear of God, it will
be less to be awed by him than to be afraid of him.* I
would like it as well, said a wise man, if my pupil spent

* Pens. Philosoph.[45]

his time playing court tennis; at least his body would be more fit.[46] I know children must be kept busy and that, for them, idleness is the danger most to be feared. What then should they learn? That is surely a noble question! Let them learn what they ought to do as men,* and not what they ought to forget.

---

* Such was the education of the Spartans according to the greatest of their kings. It is, says Montaigne, worthy of great consideration that the excellent regulations of Lycurgus, in truth monstrously perfect, were concerned with the sustenance of children as if this were their main care; and in the very homeland of the Muses, so little mention is made of doctrine that it is as if those noble youths disdained all other yokes, and, instead of our teachers of science, could only be given teachers of valor, prudence, and justice.

Now let us see how the same author speaks of the ancient Persians. Plato relates, he says, that the eldest son of their Royal line was educated thus: after his birth he was not given to women, but to eunuchs who, because of their virtue, had the highest influence with the King. They took charge of making his body handsome and healthy, and at the age of seven taught him to ride and hunt. When he reached fourteen, they placed him in the hands of four men: the wisest, most just, most temperate, and most valiant in the nation. The first taught him religion; the second to be always truthful; the third to conquer his cupidity; the fourth to fear nothing. All, I will add, were to make him good, none to make him learned.

Astyges, in Xenophon, asks Cyrus to give an account of his last lesson. It is this, he says: in our school a big boy with a small tunic gave it to one of his smaller schoolmates, and took away the latter's tunic, which was bigger. When our tutor made me judge of this dispute, I ruled that things should be left in this condition since both parties seemed to be better fitted in this way. Whereupon I was reproved for having done wrong, for I had stopped to consider suitability when I should first have provided for justice, which demands that no one be compelled in matters concerning his belongings.

Our gardens are adorned with statues and our galleries with paintings. What would you think these masterpieces of art, exhibited for public admiration, represent? The defenders of the country? or those even greater men who have enriched it by their virtues? No. They are pictures of all the aberrations of the heart and mind, carefully drawn from ancient mythology and presented to our children's curiosity at an early age—doubtless so that they may have models of bad actions before their eyes even before they know how to read.

What brings about all these abuses if not the disastrous inequality introduced among men by the distinction of talents and the debasement of virtues? That is the most evident effect of all our studies and the most dangerous of all their consequences. One no longer asks if a man is upright, but rather if he is talented; nor of a book if it is useful, but if it is well written. Rewards are showered on the witty, and virtue is left without honors. There are a thousand prizes for noble discourses, none for noble actions. But let someone tell me whether the glory attached to the best of the discourses which will be crowned by this Academy is comparable to the merit of having founded the prize?

The wise man does not chase after riches, but he is not insensitive to glory, and when he sees it so poorly distributed, his virtue, which a little emulation would have animated and made useful to society, languishes and dies out in misery and oblivion. In the long run, this is what must everywhere be the result of the prefer-

---

And he says that he was punished for it, just as we are punished in our villages for having forgotten the first aorist tense of τύπτω.[47] My schoolmaster would have to give me a fine harangue, *in genere demonstrativo*, before he could persuade me that his school matches that one.[48]

ence given to pleasing talents rather than useful ones, and what experience since the revival of the sciences and arts has only too well confirmed. We have physicists, geometers, chemists, astronomers, poets, musicians, painters; we no longer have citizens; or if a few of them are left, dispersed in our abandoned countryside, they perish there indigent and despised. Such is the condition to which those who give us bread and who give milk to our children are reduced, and such are the sentiments we have for them.

I admit, however, that the evil is not as great as it could have become. By placing healthful herbs beside various harmful plants, and by placing within several injurious animals the antidote for their wounds, eternal providence has taught sovereigns, who are its ministers, to imitate its wisdom. Following this example, that Great Monarch,[49] whose glory will only acquire new luster from age to age, drew out of the very bosom of the sciences and arts, sources of a thousand disorders, those famed societies simultaneously responsible for the dangerous trust of human knowledge and the sacred trust of morals—trusts which these societies protect by the attention they give both to maintaining within themselves the total purity of their trusts, and to requiring such purity of the members they admit.

These wise institutions, reinforced by his august successor and imitated by all the Kings of Europe, will at least serve as a check on men of letters, all of whom, in aspiring to the honor of being admitted to academies, will keep watch over themselves and try to make themselves worthy by means of useful works and irreproachable morals. Those academies which will choose, for the prize competitions honoring literary merit, subjects suited to revive love of virtue in the hearts of citizens, will show that such love reigns among them, and will give the people that very rare and sweet pleasure of seeing learned societies devote themselves to disseminating throughout the human race not merely pleasant enlightenment but also salutary teachings.

Do not, therefore, raise an objection which for me is only a new proof. So many precautions show only too well the necessity of taking them, and remedies are not sought for nonexistent evils. Why must even these, by their inadequacy, have the character of ordinary remedies? So many establishments created for the benefit of the learned are thereby all the more able to deceive concerning the objects of the sciences and to direct minds toward their cultivation. It seems, to judge by the precautions taken, that there are too many farmers and that a lack of philosophers is feared. I do not want to attempt here a comparison between agriculture and philosophy; it would not be tolerated. I shall only ask: what is philosophy? What do the writings of the best known philosophers contain? What are the teachings of these lovers of wisdom? To listen to them, would one not take them for a troop of charlatans, each crying from his own spot on a public square: Come to me, I alone do not deceive. One holds that there are no bodies and that everything is appearance. Another that there is no substance other than matter, nor any God but the world. This one suggests that there are neither virtues nor vices and that moral good and evil are chimeras. That one that men are wolves and can devour one another with clear conscience.[50] O great philosophers, why don't you save these profitable lessons for your friends and children; you would soon reap the reward, and we would have no fear of finding among ourselves any of your followers.

Such are the marvelous men on whom the esteem of their contemporaries was showered during their lifetime and for whom immortality was reserved after their death! Such are the wise maxims we have received from them and that we will transmit from age to age to our descendants. Has paganism, abandoned to all the aberrations of human reason, left posterity anything to compare with the shameful monuments prepared for it by printing under the reign of the Gospel? The impious writings of Leucippus and Diagoras died with them. The art of perpetuating the extravagances of the human mind had not yet been invented. But thanks to typography* and the use we make of it, the dangerous dreams

---

*Considering the awful disorders printing has already caused in Europe, and judging the future by the progress that this evil makes day by day, one can easily predict that sovereigns will not delay in taking as many pains to banish this terrible art from their States as they once took to establish it. The Sultan Achmet, bowing to the importunities of some supposed men of taste, had consented to establish a printing press at Constantinople. But the press had hardly begun to operate when it had to be destroyed and the equipment thrown in a well. It is said that Caliph Omar, consulted on what should be done with the library of Alexandria, replied in these terms: If the books in this library contain things opposed to the Koran, they are bad and must be burned. If they contain only the doctrine of the Koran, burn them anyway—they are superfluous. Our learned men have cited this reasoning as the height of absurdity. However, imagine Gregory the Great in place of Omar, and the Gospel in place of the Koran, the library would still have been burned, and it would be perhaps the finest deed in the life of that illustrious pontiff.

of Hobbes and Spinoza will remain forever. Go, famous writings of which the ignorance and simplicity of our forefathers would have been incapable; escort to our descendants those even more dangerous works which reek of the corruption of morals in our century, and together carry to coming centuries a faithful history of the progress and advantages of our sciences and arts. If they read you, you will not leave them any doubt about the question we discuss today; and unless they be more foolish than we, they will raise their hands to heaven and say with bitterness of heart: "Almighty God, thou who holds all spirits in thy hands, deliver us from the enlightenment and fatal arts of our forefathers, and give back to us ignorance, innocence, and poverty, the only goods that can give us happiness and are precious in thy sight."

But if the development of the sciences and arts has added nothing to our true felicity, if it has corrupted our morals, and if the corruption of morals has impaired purity of taste, what shall we think of that crowd of elementary authors who have removed the difficulties that blocked access to the temple of the muses and that nature put there as a test of strength for those who might be tempted to learn? What shall we think of those compilers of works who have indiscreetly broken down the door of the sciences and let into their sanctuary a populace unworthy of approaching it; whereas it would be preferable for all who could not go far in the learned profession to be rebuffed from the outset and directed into arts useful to society. He who will be a bad versifier or a subaltern geometer all his life would perhaps have become a great cloth maker. Those whom nature destined to be her disciples needed no teachers. Verulam,[51] Descartes, Newton, these preceptors of the human race had none themselves; indeed, what guides would have led them as far as their vast genius carried them? Ordinary teachers would only have restricted their understanding by confining it within the narrow capacity of their own. The first obstacles taught them to exert themselves, and they did their utmost to traverse the immense space they covered. If a few men must be allowed to devote themselves to the study of the sciences and arts, it must be only those who feel the strength to walk alone in their footsteps and go beyond them. It is for these few to raise monuments to the glory of human intellect. But if we wish nothing to be beyond their genius, nothing must be beyond their hopes. That is the only encouragement they need. The soul gradually adapts itself to the objects that occupy it, and it is great events that make great men. The prince of eloquence was Consul of Rome, and the greatest, perhaps, of philosophers Chancellor of England.[52] If the one had held only a chair in some university and the other obtained only a modest pension from an Academy, can it be believed, I say, that their work would not have reflected their status? Therefore may Kings not disdain to allow into their councils the men most capable of advising them well; may they renounce the old prejudice, invented by the pride of the great, that the art of leading people is more difficult than that of enlightening them, as if it were easier to engage men to do good willingly than to constrain them to do it by force. May learned men of the first rank find honorable asylum in their courts. May they obtain there the only recompense worthy of them: that of contributing by their influence to the happiness of the people to whom they will have taught wisdom. Only then will one see what can be done by virtue, science, and authority, animated by noble emulation and working together for the felicity of the human race. But so long as power is alone on the one side, intellect and wisdom alone on the other, learned men will rarely think of great things, Princes will more rarely do noble ones, and the people will continue to be vile, corrupt, and unhappy.

As for us, common men not endowed by heaven with such great talents and not destined for so much glory, let us remain in our obscurity. Let us not chase after a reputation which would escape us, and which in the present state of things would never be worth what it cost, even if we had all the qualifications to obtain it. What good is it to seek our happiness in the opinion of another if we can find it within ourselves? Let us leave to others the care of informing peoples of their duties, and limit ourselves to fulfilling well our own. We do not need to know more than this.

O virtue! sublime science of simple souls, are so many difficulties and preparations needed to know you? Are not your principles engraved in all hearts, and is it not enough in order to learn your laws to commune with oneself and listen to the voice of one's conscience in the silence of the passions? That is true philosophy, let us know how to be satisfied with it; and without envying the glory of those famous men who are immortalised in the republic of letters, let us try to put between them and us that glorious distinction noted between two great peoples long ago: that the one knew how to speak well, the other to act well.[53]

Editor's Notes to the First Discourse

1. From Ovid's *Tristia*, Book V, Elegy X.37: "Here I am the barbarian, because no one understands me." Since Rousseau considered the epigraph the clue to an entire work (see *Rousseau Juge de Jean-Jacques*, Dialogue iii [Pléiade, I, 941]), it is wise to look up the source of his preliminary quotations and compare them to the works they introduce. This quotation apparently symbolizes Rousseau's expectation that few men of his time will understand the thesis proposed in the *First Discourse*. The epigraph is, however, subtler than that: even though the arts and sciences appear to be generally condemned in the *First Discourse*, Rousseau identifies himself with Ovid, the poet, from the very outset.

2. This Foreword was added by Rousseau in 1763, when he was preparing a collected edition of his writings. It is not certain which works Rousseau includes in this unfavorable comparison—see Havens, *Rousseau: Discours sur les Sciences et les Arts*, pp. 169-70. Although Rousseau admitted elsewhere that the *First Discourse* was poorly written (*Confessions*, Book viii [Pléiade, I, 352]), he included it, together with the *Second Discourse*, among his "principal writings" (Letter to Malesherbes, Jan. 12, 1762, *Correspondance Générale de J. J. Rousseau*, ed. Théophile Dufour [20 vols.; Paris: Librairie Armand Colin, 1924-34], VII, 51).

3. When the Parlement of Paris, on June 9, 1762, condemned Rousseau's *Émile* and ordered him seized, Rousseau was forced to flee the French capital. Later that month, both the *Émile* and the *Social Contract* were condemned and burned in Geneva, where Rousseau's arrest was also ordered. Having taken refuge at Yverdon, he was forced to move early in July by a decree of the government

of Berne, and he settled in Motiers (where this Foreword was written). In September, 1765, Rousseau fled Motiers after his house was stoned; the remaining years of his life were punctuated by repeated displacements, which Rousseau often believed were necessary to avoid what he considered to be a plot against him.

4. The League (or Holy League) was an organization of French Catholics that attempted to suppress Protestants in France during the wars of religion in the sixteenth century. Formed in 1576, it ceased to be important after the victories of Henry IV and his abjuration of Protestantism in 1593.

5. There has been disagreement concerning the location of these additions. See Havens, pp. 175-76.

6. "We are deceived by the appearance of right." Horace, *On the Art of Poetry*, v. 25.

7. Note that in restating the question, Rousseau changes it. The French word *moeurs*, here translated as "morals," poses a most difficult problem for a translator. Allan Bloom has suggested "manners [morals]" as a means of conveying the combination of an ethical assessment and a description of habits implicit in the term. See *Politics and the Arts*, pp. 149-50. Although the phrase "way of life" is perhaps the best single equivalent for *moeurs*, it is awkward and does not always capture the specific nuance intended; in addition, it could be confused with the phrase *manière de vivre*, which occurs several times in the *Second Discourse*. Throughout the present translation the following convention will be adopted: when *moeurs*, in the context, has a predominantly ethical implication, it will be rendered as "morals"; when it describes usages and manners, "customs" will be used. The adoption of different English words to translate a given French term is virtually inescapable, and is justified by the following remark of Rousseau: "There is no language rich enough to furnish as many terms, nuances, and expressions as the modifications ideas can have. . . . I am convinced that one can be clear even in the

poverty of our language, not by always giving the same meanings to the same words, but by so doing that as often as each word is used, the meaning given to it is sufficiently determined by the related ideas, so that each sentence in which this word is found serves, so to speak, as its definition." *Émile*, Book ii (Hachette, II, 76). For a somewhat different translation, see Barbara Foxley, trans., *Émile* (Everyman's Library; London: J. M. Dent & Sons, n.d.), p. 72.

8. Rousseau uses *lumières* in the sense of "natural or acquired intellectual capacity." Except for several places where it is appropriate, "lights" (the literal equivalent) has been avoided as too awkward. Where the emphasis in the text seems to be primarily on man's *natural* mental faculties, "intellect" has been used; when Rousseau seems to mean primarily *acquired* intelligence, we have adopted "enlightenment." This should not cause any confusion, since the nouns "enlightenment" and "intellect" are used for no other French word (although we do translate the verb *éclairer* by the verb forms of "enlighten").

9. This sentence has a broad element of irony, as will be seen by comparing the *Second Discourse*, especially pp. 163-68. For example, note Rousseau's remark that "in relations between one man and another . . . the worst that can happen to one is to see himself at the discretion of the other" (p. 163).

10. Constantinople was captured by the Crusaders in 1203, and by the Turks in 1453 (see Havens, p. 180).

11. "The art of disputation on all things, without ever taking a stand other than to suspend one's judgment, is called *Pyrrhonism*." Pierre Bayle, *Dictionnaire historique et critique* (3rd ed.; Rotterdam: Michel Bohm, 1720), III, 2306. Compare Bayle's footnote B on that page with Rousseau's "Profession de foi du vicaire Savoyard" in Book iv of the *Émile* (in the Everyman's edition, pp. 228-78, esp. pp. 230-31).

12. This citation is from Montaigne's essay "On the Art

of Conversing," *Essays*, Book III, chapter viii. For an English translation, see the edition of Jacob Zeitlin. (3 vols.; New York: Alfred A. Knopf, 1936), III, 129. The exception is generally assumed to have been Diderot, then Rousseau's closest friend (Havens, pp. 187-88).

13. With an oratorical flourish, Rousseau alludes to the discovery, first widely accepted in the eighteenth century, that the tides are determined by the position of the moon (Havens, p. 189).

14. Although several Egyptian kings had this name, the Sesostris said to have conquered the world is apparently legendary (see Havens, p. 190).

15. Cambyses II, King of Persia, successfully invaded Egypt in 525 B.C. (Havens, p. 190).

16. King Philip of Macedonia conquered the main Greek city-states in 338 B.C. (Havens, p. 191).

17. The great Athenian orator (385?-322 B.C.) was a leading opponent of Macedonian hegemony in Greece.

18. Ennius (239 to c. 170 B.C.) was an early Latin poet, and Terence (194 to 159 B.C.) a famous author of comedies (Havens, p. 192).

19. According to Tacitus, *Annals* XVI. 18, this title (*"elegantae arbiter"*) was given to Petronius, satiric author and courtier of Nero. Since Petronius lived in the first century A.D., the "fall" of Rome under the "yoke she had imposed on so many peoples" cannot be the capture of Rome by the barbarian general Odoacer in 476 A.D. Although this event is traditionally called the "fall of Rome," it would appear that the "yoke" Rousseau has in mind is one-man rule—that is, the establishment of the Roman Empire by Augustus in the years following the Battle of Actium (31 B.C.). If this conjecture is correct—and it seems inescapable, since Rousseau speaks of the "fall" of Rome as coming *before* the day on which Petronius was called "Arbiter of Good Taste"—this passage serves as a carefully guarded equation of monarchy with subjection

or slavery. Indeed, if one considers Rousseau's examples carefully, it will be seen that states with healthy morals were often republics whereas the corrupt societies he names were mainly (though not exclusively) empires and monarchies.

20. Xenophon's *Cyropaedia* (Havens, p. 196).

21. Tacitus (c. 55 to c. 117 A.D.), especially in his *De moribus Germanorum* (Havens, p. 197).

22. The reference is to Montaigne's "Of Cannibals," *Essays*, Book I, chapter xxxi (Zeitlin, I, 181-90). Havens identifies this and other references to Montaigne in his notes.

23. Compare Montaigne, "Of Experience," *Essays*, Book III, chapter xiii (Zeitlin, I, 266).

24. Pisistratus, tyrant of Athens from 554 to 527 B.C., was reputed to have been the first to transcribe and organize the poetry of Homer, the "prince of poets" (Havens, pp. 200-201).

25. Compare Thucydides, *History of the Peloponnesian War*, I, x: "For I suppose if Lacedaemon were to become desolate, and the temples and the foundations of the public buildings were left, that as time went on there would be a strong disposition with posterity to refuse to accept her fame as a true exponent of her power. And yet they occupy two-fifths of the Peloponnese and lead the whole, not to speak of their numerous allies without. Still, as the city is neither built in a compact form nor adorned with magnificent temples and public edifices, but composed of villages after the old fashion of Hellas, there would be an impression of inadequacy. Whereas, if Athens were to suffer the same misfortune, I suppose that any inference from the appearance presented to the eye would make her power to have been twice as great as it is." (Everyman's Library; New York: E. P. Dutton & Co., 1910), p. 7.

26. For some of the implications of this paraphrase of Plato's *Apology*, see the Introduction (p. 8, n. 9).

27. Cato the Elder (234 to 149 B.C.), Roman states-
man known for his efforts to restore what he considered to
be the pure morals of the early Republic. Note that Cato
was a contemporary of Ennius, identified in note 18.
28. Epicurus (c. 342 to 270 B.C.) founded the Epicurean philosophic school or sect, and his contemporary
Zeno founded that of the Stoics; Arcesilas (316 to 241
B.C.) was an extreme skeptic who took the position that
"nothing was certain" (Havens, p. 203).
29. Havens indicates (p. 203) that Rousseau here
transcribes a sentence of Seneca ("*Postquam docti prodie-
runt, boni desunt.*" *Letters* xcv. 13), which had been
quoted by Montaigne in "Of Pedantry," *Essays*, Book I,
chapter xxv (Zeitlin, I, 122).
30. As Havens points out (p. 207), the reference here
is to Plutarch's "Life of Pyhrrus," which describes both
Cineas and Fabricius. See *Lives of the Noble Grecians and
Romans* (New York: Modern Library, n.d.), p. 481 f.
31. The irony of this rhetorical question is clear if one
considers the last sentence of Fabricius' speech: neither
King Louis XII nor King Henry IV would have been likely
to conclude that "the most noble sight that has ever appeared beneath the heavens" was the Roman Senate.
32. Compare the story told by Socrates in Plato's *Phae-
drus*, 274c-275b, concerning the origin of writing.
33. This is almost a word-for-word quotation of the
version of the fable given by Plutarch, except that Rousseau neglects to add the remainder of Prometheus' advice to
the satyr: "It burns when one touches it, but it gives light
and warmth, and is an implement serving all crafts providing one knows how to use it well." See Havens, p. 209,
and compare Plutarch, "How to Profit by One's Enemies," trans. Frank Cole Babbitt, *Moralia* (Loeb Classical
Library; London: Heinemann, 1928), II, 7-9. Note how
Rousseau strengthens his case by omitting half of the rele-

vant passage! On the fable of Prometheus, compare Plato's
Protagoras, 320d-322a.

34. Reproduced p. 30.

35. This is a difficult sentence. Although it may merely
allude to Democritus' view, quoted by Montaigne, that
truth is "hidden at the bottom of an abyss" (see Havens, p.
211), it may not be entirely fanciful to see also a reference
to Plato's allegory of the cave (*Republic* VII. 514a-521b).

36. I am indebted to Professor Joseph Cropsey for the
suggestion that, of this list of scientific discoveries due to
"illustrious philosophers," the first three refer to the work
of Newton, the next two to Descartes' philosophy, and the
last two to studies by Bacon. Compare the three philosophers mentioned by name on p. 63.

37. Compare Montesquieu, *The Spirit of the Laws*,
XXIII, xvii: "Sir [William] Petty supposed, in his calculations, that a man in England is worth what he could be sold
for in Algiers. That can only be true for England: there
are countries where a man is worth nothing; there are some
where he is worth less than nothing." (Paris: Garnier
Frères, 1949), II, 114-15. The standard English translation
is by Thomas Nugent (New York: Hafner Publishing
Company, 1949). Montesquieu's reference is to Sir William Petty's *Essay in Political Arithmetick*, published in
1686.

38. In order, Rousseau apparently refers to the conquest
of Persia by Alexander the Great (334-330 B.C.); the in-
ability of the Persians to conquer the Scythians (see especially the account of the invasion, led by Darius
Hystaspis in 512 B.C., in Herodotus, *Histories* IV. 118-
142); Rome's conquest of Carthage in the Three Punic
Wars (265-241 B.C., 218-202 B.C., and 150-146 B.C. respectively); the invasion and conquest of Rome by the Goths.
Huns and Vandals which culminated in the "fall of Rome"
to Odoacer in 476 A.D.; the conquest of the Gauls by the
Franks and the Saxon invasions of Britain in the fifth

century A.D.; the victories of the Swiss over the Austrian Hapsburgs Leopold I (1315) and Leopold III (1386), and over Charles the Bold, Duke of Burgundy (1476); and finally the successful revolt of the Netherlands against King Philip II of Spain (1566-1579). These historical references are particularly interesting because of the element of exaggeration present in many of them. The first example (the conquest of "The Monarchy of Cyrus" by an army of 30,000 men under a "prince who was poorer than the least significant Persian satrap") can only refer to the ultimate defeat of the Achaemenian dynasty founded by Cyrus the Great, since Persia was never conquered during the reign of Cyrus himself (although Cyrus was killed while fighting the Massagetae, a savage tribe east of the Caspian). Rousseau's statement of the event thus tends to mislead the hasty reader, who will not immediately recognize that Alexander the Great had become master of Greece before attacking Persia. Similarly, although Rome was not as wealthy as Carthage prior to its victory in the Punic Wars, the Roman republic was hardly "nothing" at the time; and the "handful of herring-fishers" who defeated Spain were the extremely prosperous Dutch, whose development of commerce and industry formed an indispensible basis for the successful revolt of the Northern Provinces of the Netherlands.

39. The reference is clearly to Plato's *Republic*, especially 451c–457c (where Socrates argues that the education and activities of women must equal those of men in the best city).

40. Rousseau here complains about the poor taste of French (and especially Parisian) society, with particular emphasis on the growing dislike of the classical dramas of Corneille and Racine, and the refusal to accept—or even listen seriously to—Italian music (see Havens, pp. 244-45).

41. François Marie Arouet (1694-1788), universally

known as Voltaire. Rousseau's refusal to cite the most famous author of his time by his pen name is, in this context, hardly accidental; to be famous in eighteenth-century France, Rousseau implies, one must put on a false front. Compare Havens, pp. 225-26.

42. Charles-André ("Carle") Vanloo (1705-1765) and Jean-Baptiste-Marie Pierre (1713-1789) were famous contemporary painters whose works were sometimes criticized by Diderot (Havens, pp. 226-27).

43. Jean-Baptiste Pigalle (1714-1785), French sculptor whose statues were in fashion at the time of the writing of the First Discourse (Havens, p. 228). The relative obscurity of these contemporaries named by Rousseau would seem to confirm his point that to gain fame in a corrupted society one must sacrifice those qualities which produce lasting fame.

44. Michel de Montaigne. The preceding two sentences, as well as the remainder of this one, are taken virtually word for word from Montaigne's "Of Pedantry" (Zeitlin, I, 125).

45. Rousseau thus cites Diderot's anonymous work, Pensées Philosophiques, in which the distinction between awe of God and fear of God is made in Pensée viii (see Havens, pp. 234-36). It should be noted that shortly after its publication in 1746, Pensées Philosophiques was condemned and burned by the Parlement of Paris as "scandalous, and contrary to Religion and Morals." Arthur M. Wilson, Diderot: the Testing Years (New York: Oxford University Press, 1957), p. 55.

46. Rousseau again borrows from Montaigne's "Of Pedantry" (Zeitlin, I, 120).

47. Montaigne puns here by using the Greek verb "to strike" or "beat" as his example.

48. All of this long note, with the exception of the first and last sentences of the first two paragraphs, is quoted from Montaigne's "Of Pedantry" (Zeitlin, I, 123-24).

Rousseau changes the order of the paragraphs, however, and makes one significant omission.

49. Louis XIV, King of France from 1643 to 1715, founded at least five academies: Académie Royale des Beaux-Arts (1648), Académie des Inscriptions et Belles-Lettres (1663), Académie d'Architecture (1671), Académie des Beaux-Arts at Rome (1677), and Académie des Jeux Floraux (1694). The first and most important, however, was the *Académie française*, formally constituted in 1635 under Louis XIII; *le grand monarque* (as Louis XIV was called) did not originate the institution for which he is praised. This hollow commendation of Louis XIV is paralleled by a similar instance of "damning with false praise" in the *Second Discourse*.

50. It may be suggested that the foregoing sentences allude, respectively, to Berkeley (1685-1753), Spinoza (1632-1677), Mandeville (c. 1670-1733), and Hobbes (1588-1679).

51. Francis Bacon, first Baron Verulam and Viscount St. Albans (1561-1626), who received his title after becoming Lord Chancellor of England in 1618.

52. The reference is to Cicero and Bacon. Note that Rousseau's earlier reference to the latter as "Verulam" is not accidental—compare note 51.

53. This comparison between Sparta and Athens is also drawn from Montaigne's "Of Pedantry" (Zeitlin, I, 124).

He goes back to his equals.
See note (p), pp. 225-26.

DISCOURSE

ON THE ORIGIN AND FOUNDATIONS OF INEQUALITY AMONG MEN

BY JEAN-JACQUES ROUSSEAU
CITIZEN OF GENEVA

Non in depravatis, sed in his quae bene secundum naturam se habent, considerandum est quid sit naturale.

ARISTOTLE, Politics, L.1[1]

AMSTERDAM

MARC MICHEL REY

MDCCLV

[1] The editor's footnotes to the *Second Discourse* are on pp. 229-48.

TO
THE REPUBLIC
OF GENEVA

MAGNIFICENT, MOST HONORED AND SOVEREIGN LORDS,

Being convinced that only the virtuous citizen may properly give his fatherland those honors which it may acknowledge, I have worked for thirty years to deserve to offer you public homage; and as this happy occasion partially supplements what my efforts have been unable to accomplish, I believed I might be permitted here to follow the zeal that prompts me, rather than the right that ought to be my authorization.[2] Having had the good fortune to be born among you, how could I meditate upon the equality nature established among men, and upon the inequality they have instituted, without thinking of the profound wisdom with which both, happily combined in this State, contribute, in the manner most approximate to natural law and most favorable to society, to the maintenance of public order and the happiness of individuals? While seeking the best maxims that good sense could dictate concerning the constitution of a government, I was so struck to see them all in practice in yours that even had I not been born within your walls, I should have believed myself unable to dispense with offering this picture of human society to that people which, of all others, seems to me to possess society's greatest advantages and to have best prevented its abuses.

If I had to choose my birthplace, I would have

chosen a society of a size limited by the extent of human faculties—that is, limited by the possibility of being well governed—and where, each being adequate to his job, no one would have been constrained to commit to others the functions with which he was charged; a state where, all the individuals knowing one another, neither the obscure maneuvers of vice nor the modesty of virtue could be hidden from the notice and judgment of the public, and where that sweet habit of seeing and knowing one another turned love of the fatherland into love of the citizens rather than love of the soil.

I would have wished to be born in a country where the sovereign and the people could have only one and the same interest, so that all movements of the machine always tended only to the common happiness. Since that would not be possible unless the people and the sovereign were the same person, it follows that I would have wished to be born under a democratic government, wisely tempered.

I would have wished to live and die free, that is to say so subject to the laws that neither I nor anyone else could shake off their honorable yoke: that salutary and gentle yoke, which the proudest heads bear with all the more docility because they are suited to bear no other.

I would therefore have wished that no one in the State could declare himself above the law and that no one outside could impose any law the State was obliged to recognize. For whatever the constitution of a government may be, if a single man is found who is not subject to the law, all the others are necessarily at his discretion (a); and if there is a national chief and

_____
(a) Rousseau's notes to the *Second Discourse* will be found on pp. 182-228.

another foreign chief, whatever division of authority they may make, it is impossible for both of them to be well obeyed and for the state to be well governed.

I would not have wished to live in a newly instituted republic, however good its laws might be, for fear that—the government, perhaps constituted otherwise than would be necessary for the moment, and being unsuited to the new citizens or the citizens to the new government—the State would be subject to be disturbed and destroyed almost from its birth. For freedom is like those solid and rich foods or those hearty wines, which are proper to nourish and fortify robust constitutions habituated to them, but which overpower, ruin, and intoxicate the weak and delicate who are unsuited for them. Once peoples are accustomed to masters, they are no longer able to do without them. If they try to shake off the yoke, they move all the farther away from freedom because, mistaking for freedom an unbridled license which is its opposite, their revolutions almost always deliver them to seducers who only make their chains heavier. The Roman people itself, that model of all free peoples, was not capable of governing itself on emerging from the oppression of the Tarquins. Debased by slavery and the ignominious labors the Tarquins had imposed on it, it was at first only a stupid mob that needed to be handled and governed with the greatest wisdom, so that, growing accustomed little by little to breathe the salutary air of freedom, those souls, enervated or rather brutalized under tyranny, acquired by degrees that severity of morals and that spirited courage which eventually made them the most respectable of all peoples. I would therefore have sought for my fatherland a happy and tranquil Republic, whose antiquity was in a way lost in the darkness of time, which had experienced only those attacks suited to display and strengthen courage and love of fatherland in its inhabitants, and where the citizens, long accustomed to prudent independence, were not only free but worthy of being so.

I would have wished to choose for myself a fatherland diverted by its fortunate impotence from the fierce love of conquests, and safeguarded by an even more fortunate location from the fear of becoming itself the conquest of another State; a free city, situated among several peoples none of whom had an interest in invading it, while each had an interest in preventing the others from invading it themselves; in a word, a Republic that did not tempt the ambition of its neighbors, and that could reasonably count on their help if necessary. It follows that, in such a fortunate position, it would have had nothing to fear except from itself; and that, if its citizens were trained in the use of arms, it would have been to maintain in them that warlike ardor and that spirited courage which suit freedom so well and whet the appetite for it, rather than from the necessity to provide for their own defense.

I would have sought a country where the right of legislation was common to all citizens; for who can know better than they under what conditions it suits them to live together in the same society? But I would not have approved of plebiscites like those of the Romans, where the chiefs of the State and those most interested in its preservation were excluded from the deliberations on which its safety often depended, and where, by an absurd inconsistency, the magistrates were deprived of the rights enjoyed by the ordinary citizens.

On the contrary, I would have desired that, in order to stop the selfish and ill-conceived projects and the dangerous innovations that finally ruined the Athenians, everyone did not have the power to propose new laws according to his fancy; that this right belonged exclusively to the magistrates; that even they used it with so much caution that the people, on its side, was so hesitant in giving its consent to these laws, and that their promulgation could only be done with so much solemnity, that before the constitution was shaken one had time to be convinced that it is above all the great antiquity of laws which makes them holy and venerable; that the people soon scorns those laws which it sees change daily; and that in growing accustomed to neglect old usages on the pretext of making improvements, great evils are often introduced to correct lesser ones.

Above all I would have fled, as necessarily ill-governed, a Republic where the people, believing it could do without its magistrates or only allow them a precarious authority, would imprudently have retained the administration of civil affairs and the execution of its own laws. Such must have been the rude constitution of the first governments emerging immediately out of the state of nature, and such was also one of the vices that ruined the Republic of Athens.

Rather I would have chosen that Republic where the individuals, being content to give sanction to the laws and to decide in a body and upon the report of their chiefs the most important public affairs, would establish respected tribunals, distinguish with care their various departments, elect from year to year the most capable and most upright of their fellow citizens to administer justice and govern the State; and where, the virtue of the magistrates thus being evidence of the wisdom of the people, they would mutually honor each other. So that if ever some fatal misunderstandings happened to disturb public concord, even those times of blindness and errors were marked by proofs of moderation, reciprocal esteem, and a common respect for the laws: presages and guarantees of a sincere and perpetual reconciliation.[3]

Such are, MAGNIFICENT, MOST HONORED, AND SOVEREIGN LORDS, the advantages that I would have sought in the fatherland I would have chosen for myself. And if Providence had in addition given it a charming site, a temperate climate, a fertile countryside, and the most delightful appearance beneath the heavens, to complete my happiness I would have desired only to enjoy all these things in the bosom of that happy fatherland, living peacefully in sweet society with my fellow citizens, practicing toward them, and following their example, humanity, friendship, and all the virtues; and leaving behind me the honorable memory of a good man and a decent and virtuous patriot.

If, less happy or too late wise, I saw myself reduced to end an infirm and languishing career in other climes, uselessly regretting the repose and peace of which my imprudent youth deprived me, I would at least have nourished in my soul those same sentiments I could not use in my fatherland; and moved by a tender and disinterested affection for my distant fellow citizens, from the bottom of my heart I would have addressed to them approximately the following discourse:

My dear fellow citizens, or rather my brothers, since the bonds of blood as well as the laws unite almost all of us, it gives me pleasure to be unable to think of you without at the same time thinking of all the good things you enjoy, and of which perhaps none of you knows the value better than I who have lost them. The more I reflect upon your political and civil situation, the less I can imagine that the nature of human things could admit of a better one. In all other governments, when the question is to assure the greatest good of the State, everything is always limited to imaginary projects, and at most to simple possibilities. As for you, your happiness is all established, it is only necessary to enjoy it; and to become perfectly happy you have no other need than to know how to be satisfied being so. Your sovereignty, acquired or recovered at sword's point, and preserved through two centuries by dint of valor and wisdom, is at last fully and universally recognized. Honorable treaties determine your boundaries, secure your rights, and strengthen your repose. Your constitution is excellent, dictated by the most sublime reason and guaranteed by friendly and respectable powers; your State is tranquil; you have neither wars nor conquerors to fear; you have no other masters except the wise laws you have made, administered by upright magistrates of your own choice. You are neither rich enough to enervate yourself by softness and lose in vain delights the taste for true happiness and solid virtues, nor poor enough to need more foreign help than your industry procures for you. And this precious freedom, which in large nations is maintained only by exorbitant taxes, costs you almost nothing to preserve.

For the happiness of its citizens and the example of peoples, may a Republic so wisely and so happily constituted endure forever! This is the sole wish left for you to make, and the only precaution left for you to take. Henceforth it is for you alone, not to create your happiness, since your ancestors have saved you the trouble, but to make it lasting by the wisdom of using it well. It is upon your perpetual unity, your obedience to the laws, your respect for their ministers that your preservation depends. If there remains among you the least germ of bitterness or distrust, hasten to destroy it as a deadly leaven which sooner or later would result in your misfortunes and the ruin of the State. I implore all of you to look deep into your hearts and consult the secret voice of your conscience. Does anyone among you know a more upright, more enlightened, more respectable body than that of your magistracy? Do not all its members give you the example of moderation, of simplicity of morals, of respect for the laws, and of the most sincere reconciliation?⁴ Then give such wise chiefs, without reserve, that salutary confidence which reason owes to virtue; bear in mind that they are of your choice, that they justify it, and that the honors due to those whom you have established in dignity necessarily reflect upon yourselves. None of you is so unenlightened as to be ignorant that where the vigor of laws and the authority of their defenders cease, there can be neither security nor freedom for anyone. Therefore what is at issue among you except to do wholeheartedly and with just confidence what you should always be obliged to do by a true self-interest, by duty, and for the sake of reason. May a guilty and fatal indifference to the maintenance of the constitution never make you neglect in need the wise advice of the most enlightened and zealous among you; but may equity, moderation, and the most respectful firmness continue to regulate all your actions and display in you, before the whole universe, the example of a proud and modest people as jealous of its glory as of its freedom. Beware above all, and this will be my last counsel, of ever listening to sinister interpretations and venomous discourses, the secret motives of which are often more dangerous than the acts that are their object. An entire household awakes and takes warning at the first cries of a good and faithful guardian that never barks except at the approach of robbers; but people hate the importunity of those noisy animals that continually trouble public repose and whose continual and misplaced warnings are not heeded even at the moment when they are necessary.

And you, MAGNIFICENT AND MOST HONORED LORDS, you worthy and respectable magistrates of a free people,[5] permit me to offer you in particular my homages and my respects. If there is a rank in the world suited to do honor to those who hold it, it is doubtless that which is given by talents and virtue, that of which you have made yourselves worthy, and to which your fellow citizens have raised you. Their own merit adds to yours still another luster; and I find you, chosen by men capable of governing others in order that they themselves be governed, as much above other magistrates as a free people, and especially that one which you have the honor to lead, is, by its enlightenment and reason, above the populace of other States.

May I be allowed to cite an example of which better records ought to remain, and which will always be present in my heart. I never recall without the sweetest emotion the memory of the virtuous citizen to whom I owe my being, and who often spoke to me in my childhood of the respect that was due you. I see him still, living from the work of his hands, and nourishing his soul on the most sublime truths. I see Tacitus, Plutarch, and Grotius mingled with the instruments of his trade before him. I see at his side a beloved son, receiving with too little profit the tender instructions of the best of fathers.[6] But if the aberrations of foolish youth made me forget such wise lessons for a time,[7] I have the happiness to feel at last that no matter what inclination one may have toward vice, it is difficult for an education in which the heart is involved to remain forever lost.

Such are, MAGNIFICENT AND MOST HONORED LORDS, the citizens and even the simple inhabitants born in the State you govern; such are those educated and sensible men of whom, under the name of workers and common-people, those in other nations have such base and false ideas. My father, I joyfully admit it, was not distinguished among his fellow citizens: he was only what they all are; and such as he was, there is no country where his company would not have been sought after, cultivated, and even profitably, by the most respectable men. It does not behoove me and, thank heaven, it is not necessary to speak to you of the consideration which can be expected from you by men of that stamp: your equals by education as well as by the rights of nature and of birth; your inferiors by their will and by the preference they owe your merit, which they have accorded it, and for which you owe them in turn a kind of gratitude. I learn with keen satisfaction of how much you temper toward them, by gentleness and condescension, the gravity suited to ministers of the laws; how much you return to them in esteem and attentions what they owe you in obedience and respects: conduct full of justice and wisdom, suited to put farther and farther away the memory of the unhappy events which must be forgotten in order that they never be seen again;[8] conduct all the more judicious as this equitable and generous people makes a pleasure of its duty, as it naturally loves to honor you, and as the most ardent in upholding their rights are the most inclined to respect yours.

It ought not to be surprising that the chiefs of a civil society love its glory and happiness; but it is too much so for the repose of men that those who consider themselves as the magistrates, or rather as the masters, of a more holy and more sublime fatherland indicate some love for the terrestrial fatherland which nourishes them.[9] How sweet it is for me to be able to make such a rare exception in our favor, and to place in the rank of our best citizens those zealous trustees of the sacred dogmas authorized by the laws, those venerable pastors of souls, whose lively and sweet eloquence carries the maxims of the Gospel the better into hearts as the pastors always begin by practicing them themselves. Everyone knows with what success the great art of preaching is cultivated in Geneva. But as people are too accustomed to seeing things spoken of in one way and done in another, few of them know to what point the spirit of Christianity, saintliness of morals, severity to oneself and gentleness to others reign in the body of our ministers. Perhaps it behooves the city of Geneva alone to provide the edifying example of such a perfect union between a society of theologians and of men of letters; it is in great part upon their wisdom and recognized moderation, and upon their zeal for the prosperity of the State, that I ground hope for its eternal tranquillity; and I note, with a pleasure mixed with astonishment and respect, how much they abhor the atrocious maxims of those sacred and barbarous men of whom history provides more than one example, and who, in order to uphold the pretended rights of God—

that is to say their own interests—were all the less sparing of human blood because they flattered themselves that their own would always be respected.

Could I forget that precious half of the Republic which creates the happiness of the other and whose gentleness and wisdom maintain peace and good morals? Amiable and virtuous countrywomen,[10] the fate of your sex will always be to govern ours. It is fortunate when your chaste power, exercised solely in conjugal union, makes itself felt only for the glory of the State and the public happiness! Thus did women command at Sparta and thus do you deserve to command at Geneva. What barbarous man could resist the voice of honor and reason in the mouth of a tender wife? And who would not despise vain luxury seeing your simple and modest attire which, from the luster it derives from you, seems the most favorable to beauty? It is for you to maintain always, by your amiable and innocent dominion and by your insinuating wit, love of laws in the State and concord among the citizens; to reunite, by happy marriages, divided families; and above all to correct, by the persuasive sweetness of your lessons and by the modest graces of your conversation, the extravagances our young people adopt in other countries, whence, instead of the many useful things from which they could profit, they bring back, with a childish tone and ridiculous airs adopted among debauched women, only admiration for I know not what pretended grandeurs, frivolous compensations for servitude, which will never be worth as much as august freedom. Therefore always be what you are, the chaste guardians of morals and the gentle bonds of peace; and continue to exploit on every occasion the rights of the heart and of nature for the benefit of duty and virtue.

I flatter myself that events will not prove me mistaken in founding upon such guarantees hope for the general happiness of the citizens and for the glory of the Republic. I admit that with all these advantages it will not shine with that brillance which dazzles most eyes, the childish and fatal taste for which is the most mortal enemy of happiness and freedom. Let dissolute youth go to seek easy pleasures and long lasting repentance elsewhere; let the supposed men of taste admire in other places the grandeur of palaces, the beauty of carriages, the superb furnishings, the pomp of spectacles, and all the refinements of softness and luxury. In Geneva one will find only men; but such a spectacle has, nonetheless, its value, and those who seek it will be worth more than the admirers of the rest.

May you all, MAGNIFICENT, MOST HONORED, AND SOVEREIGN LORDS, deign to receive with the same goodness the respectful testimonies of the interest I take in your common prosperity. If I were unfortunate enough to be guilty of some indiscreet excess in this lively effusion of my heart, I beg you to pardon it as the tender affection of a true patriot, and as the ardent and legitimate zeal of a man who conceives no greater happiness for himself than that of seeing all of you happy.

I remain, with the most profound respect,

MAGNIFICENT, MOST HONORED AND SOVEREIGN LORDS,

Your most humble and most obedient servant and fellow citizen,

Jean-Jacques Rousseau

Chambéry
June 12, 1754

Preface

THE MOST USEFUL and least advanced of all human knowledge seems to me to be that of man (b); and I dare say that the inscription of the temple of Delphi alone contained a precept more important and more difficult than all the thick volumes of the moralists.[11] Thus I consider the subject of this Discourse one of the most interesting questions that philosophy might propose, and unhappily for us, one of the thorniest that philosophers might resolve: for how can the source of inequality among men be known unless one begins by knowing men themselves? And how will man manage to see himself as nature formed him, through all the changes that the sequence of time and things must have produced in his original constitution, and to separate what he gets from his own stock from what circumstances and his progress have added to or changed in his primitive state? Like the statue of Glaucus, which time, sea, and storms had so disfigured that it looked less like a god than a wild beast,[12] the human soul, altered in the bosom of society by a thousand continually renewed causes, by the acquisition of a mass of knowledge and errors, by changes that occurred in the constitution of bodies, and by the continual impact of the passions, has, so to speak, changed its appearance to the point of being nearly unrecognizable; and, instead of a being acting always by fixed and invariable principles, instead of that heavenly and majestic simplicity with which its author had endowed it, one no longer finds anything except the ugly contrast of passion which presumes to reason and understanding in delirium.

What is even crueler is that, as all the progress of the human species continually moves it farther away from its primitive state, the more new knowledge we accumulate, the more we deprive ourselves of the means of acquiring the most important knowledge of all; so that it is, in a sense, by dint of studying man that we have made ourselves incapable of knowing him.

It is easy to see that one must seek in these successive changes of the human constitution the first origin of the differences distinguishing men—who, by common avowal, are naturally as equal among themselves as were the animals of each species before various physical causes had introduced into certain species the varieties we notice. In effect, it is not conceivable that these first changes, by whatever means they occurred, altered all at once and in the same way all the individuals of the species; but some, being perfected or deteriorated and having acquired diverse qualities, good or bad, which were not inherent in their nature, the others remained longer in their original state. And such was the first source of inequality among men, which is more easily demonstrated thus in general than assigned its true causes with precision.

Let my readers not imagine, therefore, that I dare flatter myself with having seen what appears to me so difficult to see. I began some lines of reasoning, I ventured some conjectures, less in the hope of resolving the question than with the intention of clarifying it and reducing it to its true state. Others will easily be able to go farther on the same road, though it will not be easy for anyone to reach the end of it; for it is no light undertaking to separate what is original from what is artificial in the present nature of man, and to know correctly a state which no longer exists, which perhaps never existed, which probably never will exist, and about which it is nevertheless necessary to have precise notions in order to judge our present state correctly. He who would try to determine exactly which precautions to take in order to make solid observations on this subject would need even more philosophy than is generally thought; and a good solution of the following problem would not seem to me unworthy of the Aristotles and Plinys of our century: *What experiments would be necessary to achieve knowledge of natural man? And what are the means for making these experiments in the midst of society?* Far from undertaking to resolve this problem, I think I have pondered the subject enough to dare answer in advance that the greatest philosophers will not be too good to direct these experiments, nor the most powerful sovereigns to make them: cooperation which it is hardly reasonable to expect, especially with the perseverance or rather the succession of intellect and good will necessary, on one side and the other, to achieve success.

These researches, so difficult to conduct and so little thought of until now, are nevertheless the only means we have left to remove a multitude of difficulties that hide from us knowledge of the real foundations of human society. It is this ignorance of the nature of man that throws so much uncertainty and obscurity on the true definition of natural right: for the idea of right, says M. Burlamaqui, and even more that of natural right are manifestly ideas relative to the nature of man. It is therefore from this very nature of man, he continues, from his constitution and his state, that the principles of that science must be deduced.[13]

It is not without surprise and scandal that one notes the little agreement which prevails on this important matter among the various authors who have discussed it. Among the most serious writers one can hardly find two who are of the same opinion on this point. Without speaking of the ancient philosophers, who seem to have tried their best to contradict each other on the most fundamental principles, the Roman jurists subject man and all the other animals indifferently to the same natural law, because they consider under this name the law that nature imposes upon itself rather than that which it prescribes; or rather because of the particular sense in which those jurists understand the word *law*, which on this occasion they seem to have taken only for the expression of the general relations established by nature among all animate beings for their common preservation.[14] The moderns, recognizing under the name *law* only a rule prescribed to a moral being, that is to say, intelligent, free, and considered in his relations with other beings, consequently limit the competence of natural law to the sole animal endowed with reason, namely man; but each defining this law in his own fashion, they all establish it upon such metaphysical principles that even among us there are very few people capable of comprehending these principles, far from being able to find them by themselves.[15] So that all the definitions of these wise men, otherwise in perpetual contradiction to one another, agree only in this, that it is impossible to understand the law of nature and consequently to obey it without being a great reasoner and a profound metaphysician: which means precisely that men must have used, for the establishment of society, enlightenment which only develops with great difficulty and in very few people in the midst of society itself.

Knowing nature so little, and agreeing so poorly upon the meaning of the word *law*, it would be very difficult to agree on a good definition of natural law. Thus all those that are found in books, besides not being uniform, have in addition the fault of being drawn from several kinds of knowledge which men do not naturally have, and from advantages which men can conceive of only after having left the state of nature. Writers begin by seeking the rules on which, for the common utility, it would be appropriate that men agree among themselves; and then they give the name *natural law* to the collection of these rules, without other proof than the good which they judge would result from their universal application. This is surely a very facile way to compose definitions and to explain the nature of things by almost arbitrary conveniences.

But so long as we do not know natural man, we would try in vain to determine the law he has received or that which best suits his constitution. All that we can see very clearly concerning this law is that, for it to be law, not only must the will of him who is bound by it be able to submit to it with knowledge; but also, for it to be natural, it must speak directly by nature's voice.

Leaving aside therefore all scientific books which teach us only to see men as they have made themselves, and meditating on the first and simplest operations of the human soul, I believe I perceive in it two principles anterior to reason, of which one interests us ardently in our well-being and our self-preservation, and the other inspires in us a natural repugnance to see any sensitive being perish or suffer, principally our fellowmen. It is from the conjunction and combination that our mind is able to make of these two principles, without the necessity of introducing that of sociability,[16] that all the rules of natural right appear to me to flow: rules which reason is later forced to re-establish upon other foundations when, by its successive developments, it has succeeded in stifling nature.

In this way one is not forced to make man a philosopher before making him a man; his duties toward others are not dictated to him solely by the belated lessons of wisdom; and as long as he does not resist the inner impulse of commiseration, he will never harm another man or even another sensitive being, except in the legitimate case where, his preservation being concerned, he is obliged to give himself preference. By this means one also ends the ancient disputes about the participation of animals in natural law; for it is clear that, being devoid of intellect and freedom, they cannot recognize this law. But as they share something of our nature through the sensitivity with which they are endowed, one will judge that they too ought to participate in natural right, and that man is subject to some sort of duties toward them. It seems, in effect, that if I am obliged to do no harm to my fellow man, it is less because he is a reasonable being than because he is a sensitive being: a quality that, being common to beast and man, ought at least to give the one the right not to be uselessly mistreated by the other.

This same study of original man, of his true needs, and of the principles underlying his duties, is also the only good means one could use to remove those crowds of difficulties which present themselves concerning the origin of moral inequality, the true foundations of the body politic, the reciprocal rights of its members, and a thousand similar questions as important as they are ill explained.

When human society is considered with calm and disinterested attention, it seems to show at first only the violence of powerful men and the oppression of the weak: the mind revolts against the harshness of the former; one is prompted to deplore the blindness of the latter. And as nothing is less stable among men than those external relationships which chance produces more often than wisdom, and which are called weakness or power, wealth or poverty, human establishments appear at first glance to be founded on piles of quicksand. It is only by examining them closely, it is only after removing the dust and sand that surround the edifice, that one perceives the unshakeable base upon which it is built, and that one learns to respect its foundations. Now without serious study of man, of his natural faculties and their successive developments, one will never succeed in making such distinctions and in separating, in the present constitution of things, what divine will has done from what human art has pretended to do. The political and moral researches occasioned by the important question I examine are therefore useful in all ways; and the hypothetical history of governments is an instructive lesson for man in all respects. By considering what we would have become abandoned to ourselves, we ought to learn to bless him whose beneficent hand, correcting our institutions and giving them an unshakeable base, has prevented the disorders which must otherwise have resulted from them, and has created our happiness from the means that seemed likely to heighten our misery.

Quem te Deus esse
Jussit, et humana qua parte locatus es in re,
Disce.[17]

Notice on the Notes

I HAVE ADDED some notes to this work, following my lazy custom of working in fits and starts. These notes sometimes stray so far from the subject that they are not good to read with the text. I have therefore relegated them to the end of the Discourse, in which I have tried my best to follow the straightest path. Those who have the courage to begin again will be able to amuse themselves the second time in beating the bushes, and try to go through the notes. There will be little harm if others do not read them at all.[18]

QUESTION

Proposed by the Academy of Dijon

What is the origin of inequality
among men; and is it authorized
by natural law?

Discourse on the Origin and Foundations of Inequality Among Men[19]

IT IS OF MAN that I am to speak; and the question I examine informs me that I am going to speak to men; for such questions are not proposed by those who are afraid of honoring the truth. Therefore I shall defend with confidence the cause of humanity before the wise men who invite me to do so, and I shall not be discontent with myself if I prove myself worthy of my subject and my judges.

I conceive of two sorts of inequality in the human species: one, which I call natural or physical, because it is established by nature and consists in the difference of ages, health, bodily strengths, and qualities of mind or soul;[20] the other, which may be called moral or political inequality, because it depends upon a sort of convention and is established, or at least authorized, by the consent of men. The latter consists in the different privileges that some men enjoy to the prejudice of others, such as to be richer, more honored, more powerful than they, or even to make themselves obeyed by them.

One cannot ask what the source of natural inequality is, because the answer would be found enunciated in the simple definition of the word. Still less can one inquire if there would not be some essential link between the two inequalities; for that would be asking, in other terms, whether those who command are necessarily worth more than those who obey, and whether strength of body or mind, wisdom or virtue, are always found in the same individuals in proportion to power or wealth: a question perhaps good for slaves to discuss in the hearing of their masters, but not suitable for reasonable and free men who seek the truth.

Precisely what, then, is at issue in this Discourse? To indicate in the progress of things the moment when, right taking the place of violence, nature was subjected to law; to explain by what sequence of marvels the strong could resolve to serve the weak, and the people to buy imaginary repose at the price of real felicity.

The philosophers who have examined the foundations of society have all felt the necessity of going back to the state of nature, but none of them has reached it. Some have not hesitated to attribute to man in that state the notion of the just and unjust, without troubling themselves to show that he had to have that notion or even that it was useful to him. Others have spoken of the natural right that everyone has to preserve what belongs to him, without explaining what they meant by *belong*. Still others, giving the stronger authority over the weaker from the first, have forthwith made government arise, without thinking of the time that must have elapsed before the meaning of the words "authority" and "government" could exist among men. All of them, finally, speaking continually of need, avarice, oppression, desires, and pride, have carried over to the state of nature ideas they had acquired in society: they spoke about savage man and they described civil man. It did not even enter the minds of most of our philosophers to doubt that the state of nature had existed, even though it is evident from reading the Holy Scriptures that the first man, having received enlightenment and precepts directly from God, was not himself in that state; and that giving the writings of Moses the credence that any Christian philosopher owes them, it must be denied that even before the flood men were ever in the pure state of nature, unless they fell back into it because of some extraordinary event: a paradox that is very embarrassing to defend and altogether impossible to prove.

Let us therefore begin by setting all the facts aside, for they do not affect the question. The researches which can be undertaken concerning this subject must not be taken for historical truths, but only for hypothetical and conditional reasonings better suited to clarify the nature of things than to show their true origin, like those our physicists make every day concerning the formation of the world. Religion commands us to believe that since God Himself took men out of the state of nature immediately after the creation, they are unequal because He wanted them to be so; but it does not forbid us to form conjectures, drawn solely from the nature of man and the beings surrounding him, about what the human race might have become if it had remained abandoned to itself. That is what I am asked, and what I propose to examine in this Discourse. As my subject concerns man in general, I shall try to use a language that suits all nations, or rather, forgetting times and places in order to think only of the men to whom I speak, I shall imagine myself in the Lyceum of Athens, repeating the lessons of my masters, with Plato and Xenocrates for judges, and the human race for an audience.

O man, whatever country you may come from, whatever your opinions may be, listen: here is your history as I believed it to read, not in the books of your fellow-men, which are liars, but in nature, which never lies. Everything that comes from nature will be true; there will be nothing false except what I have involuntarily put in of my own. The times of which I am going to speak are very far off: how you have changed from what you were! It is, so to speak, the life of your species that I am going to describe to you according to the qualities you received, which your education and habits have been able to corrupt but have not been able to destroy. There is, I feel, an age at which the individual man would want to stop: you will seek the age at which you would desire your species had stopped. Discontented with your present state for reasons that foretell even greater discontents for your unhappy posterity, perhaps you would want to be able to go backward in time. This sentiment must be the eulogy of your first ancestors, the criticism of your contemporaries, and the dread of those who will have the unhappiness to live after you.

FIRST PART

Important as it may be, in order to judge the natural state of man correctly, to consider him from his origin and examine him, so to speak, in the first embryo of the species, I shall not follow his organic structure through its successive developments. I shall not stop to investigate in the animal system what he could have been at the beginning in order to become at length what he is. I shall not examine whether, as Aristotle thinks, man's elongated nails were not at first hooked claws;[21] whether he was not hairy like a bear; and whether, if he walked on all fours (c), his gaze, directed toward the earth and confined to a horizon of several paces, did not indicate both the character and the limits of his ideas. On this subject I could form only vague and almost imaginary conjectures. Comparative anatomy has as yet made too little progress and the observations of naturalists are as yet too uncertain for one to be able to establish the basis of solid reasoning upon such foundations. Thus, without having recourse to the supernatural knowledge we have on this point, and without regard to the changes that must have come about in the internal as well as external conformation of man as he applied his limbs to new uses and as he nourished himself on new foods, I shall suppose him to have been formed from all time as I see him today: walking on two feet, using his hands as we do ours, directing his gaze on all of nature, and measuring the vast expanse of heaven with his eyes.

Stripping this being, so constituted, of all the supernatural gifts he could have received and of all the artificial faculties he could only have acquired by long progress—considering him, in a word, as he must have come from the hands of nature—I see an animal less strong than some, less agile than others, but all things considered, the most advantageously organized of all. I see him satisfying his hunger under an oak, quenching his thirst at the first stream, finding his bed at the foot of the same tree that furnished his meal; and therewith his needs are satisfied.

The earth, abandoned to its natural fertility (d) and covered by immense forests never mutilated by the axe, offers at every step storehouses and shelters to animals of all species. Men, dispersed among the animals, observe and imitate their industry, and thereby develop in themselves the instinct of the beasts; with the advantage that whereas each species has only its own proper instinct, man—perhaps having none that belongs to him—appropriates them all to himself, feeds himself equally well with most of the diverse foods (*e*) which the other animals share, and consequently finds his subsistence more easily than any of them can.

Accustomed from infancy to inclemencies of the weather and the rigor of the seasons, trained in fatigue, and forced, naked and without arms, to defend their lives and their prey against other wild beasts, or to escape by outrunning them, men develop a robust and almost unalterable temperament. Children, bringing into the world the excellent constitution of their fathers and fortifying it with the same training that produced it, thus acquire all the vigor of which the human species is capable. Nature treats them precisely as the law of Sparta treated the children of citizens: it renders strong and robust those who are well constituted and makes all the others perish, thereby differing from our societies, in which the State, by making children burdensome to their fathers, kills them indiscriminately before their birth.

The savage man's body being the only implement he knows, he employs it for various uses of which, through lack of training, our bodies are incapable; our industry deprives us of the strength and agility that necessity obliges him to acquire. If he had an axe, would his wrist break such strong branches? If he had a sling, would he throw a stone so hard? If he had a ladder, would he climb a tree so nimbly? If he had a horse, would he run so fast? Give civilized man time to assemble all his machines around him and there can be no doubt that he will easily overcome savage man. But if you want to see an even more unequal fight, put them, naked and disarmed, face to face, and you will soon recognize the advantage of constantly having all of one's strength at one's disposal, of always being ready for any event, and of always carrying oneself, so to speak, entirely with one (f).

Hobbes claims that man is naturally intrepid and seeks only to attack and fight.[22] An illustrious philosopher thinks, on the contrary, and Cumberland and Pufendorf also affirm, that nothing is so timid as man in the state of nature, and that he is always trembling and ready to flee at the slightest noise he hears, at the slightest movement he perceives.[23] That may be so with respect to objects he does not know; and I do not doubt that he is frightened by all the new sights that present themselves to him every time he can neither discern the physical good and evil to be expected nor compare his forces with the dangers he must run: rare circumstances in the state of nature, where all things move in such a uniform manner, and where the face of the earth is not subject to those brusque and continual changes caused by the passions and inconstancy of united peoples. But savage man, living dispersed among the animals and early finding himself in a position to measure himself against them, soon makes the comparison; and sensing that he surpasses them in skill more than they surpass him in strength, he learns not to fear them any more. Pit a bear or a wolf against a savage who is robust, agile, courageous, as they all are, armed with stones and a good stick, and you will see that the danger will be reciprocal at the very least, and that after several similar experiences wild beasts, which do not like to attack each other, will hardly attack man willingly, having found him to be just as wild as they. With regard to animals that actually have more strength than man has skill, he is in the position of the other weaker species, which nevertheless subsist. But man has the advantage that, no less adept at running than they and finding almost certain refuge in trees, he always has the option of accepting or leaving the encounter and the choice of flight or combat. Let us add that it does not appear that any animal naturally makes war upon man except in case of self-defense or extreme hunger, or gives evidence of those violent antipathies toward him that seem to announce that one species is destined by nature to serve as food for the other.

These are, without doubt, the reasons why Negroes and savages trouble themselves so little about the wild beasts they may encounter in the woods. In this respect the Caribs of Venezuela, among others, live in the most profound security and without the slightest inconvenience. Although they go nearly naked, says François Corréal, they nevertheless expose themselves boldly in the woods armed only with bow and arrow, but no one has ever heard that any of them were devoured by beasts.

Other more formidable enemies, against which man does not have the same means of defense, are natural infirmities: infancy, old age, and illnesses of all kinds, sad signs of our weakness, of which the first two are common to all animals and the last belongs principally to man living in society. I even observe on the subject of infancy that the mother, since she carries her child with her everywhere, can nourish it with more facility than the females of several animals, which are forced to come and go incessantly with great fatigue, in one direction to seek their food and in the other to suckle or nourish their young. It is true that if the woman should die, the child greatly risks dying with her; but this danger is common to a hundred other species, whose young are for a long time unable to go and seek their nourishment themselves. And if infancy is longer among us, so also is life; everything remains approximately equal in this respect (g), although there are, concerning the duration of the first age and the number of young (h), other rules which are not within my subject. Among the aged, who act and perspire little, the need for food diminishes with the faculty of providing for it; and since savage life keeps gout and rheumatism away from them and since old age is, of all ills, the one that human assistance can least relieve, they finally die without it being perceived that they cease to be, and almost without perceiving it themselves.

With regard to illnesses, I shall not repeat the vain and false declamations against medicine made by most people in good health; rather, I shall ask whether there is any solid observation from which one might conclude that in countries where this art is most neglected, the average life of man is shorter than in those where it is cultivated with the greatest care. And how could that be, if we give ourselves more ills than medicine can furnish remedies? The extreme inequality in our way of life: excess of idleness in some, excess of labor in others; the ease of stimulating and satisfying our appetites and our sensuality; the overly refined foods of the rich, which nourish them with binding juices and overwhelm them with indigestion; the bad food of the poor, which they do not even have most of the time, so that their want inclines them to overburden their stomachs greedily when the occasion permits; late nights, excesses of all kinds, immoderate ecstasies of all the passions, fatigues and exhaustion of mind; number-less sorrows and afflictions which are felt in all conditions and by which souls are perpetually tormented: these are the fatal proofs that most of our ills are our own work, and that we would have avoided almost all of them by preserving the simple, uniform, and solitary way of life prescribed to us by nature. If nature destined us to be healthy, I almost dare affirm that the state of reflection is a state contrary to nature and that the man who meditates is a depraved animal. When one thinks of the good constitution of savages, at least of those whom we have not ruined with our strong liquors; when one learns that they know almost no illnesses except wounds and old age, one is strongly inclined to believe that the history of human illnesses could easily be written by following that of civil societies. This at least is the opinion of Plato, who judges, from certain remedies used or approved by Podalirius and Machaon at the siege of Troy, that various illnesses that should have been caused by those remedies were not yet known at that time among men;[24] and Paracelsus reports that the diet, so necessary today, was invented only by Hip-pocrates.

With so few sources of illness, man in the state of nature hardly has need of remedies, still less of doctors. In this respect the human species is not in any worse condition than all the others; and it is easy to learn from hunters whether in their chases they find many sick animals. They find many that have received extensive but very well healed wounds, that have had bones and even limbs broken and set again with no other surgeon than time, no other regimen than their ordinary life, and that are no less perfectly cured for not having been tormented with incisions, poisoned with drugs, or weakened with fasting. Finally, however useful well-administered medicine may be among us, it is still certain that if a sick savage abandoned to himself has nothing to hope for except from nature, in return he has nothing to fear except from his illness, which often renders his situation preferable to ours.

Let us therefore take care not to confuse savage man with the men we have before our eyes. Nature treats all the animals abandoned to its care with a partiality that seems to show how jealous it is of this right. The horse, the cat, the bull, even the ass, are mostly taller, and all have a more robust constitution, more vigor, more strength and courage in the forest than in our houses. They lose half of these advantages in becoming domesticated, and it might be said that all our cares to treat and feed these animals well end only in their degeneration.[25] It is the same even for man. In becoming sociable and a slave he becomes weak, fearful, servile; and his soft and effeminate way of life completes the enervation of both his strength and his courage. Let us add that between savage and domesticated conditions the difference from man to man must be still greater than that from beast to beast; for animal and man having been treated equally by nature, all the commodities of which man gives himself more than the animals he tames are so many particular causes that make him degenerate more noticeably.

Nakedness, lack of habitation, and deprivation of all those useless things we believe so necessary are not, then, such a great misfortune for these first men; nor, above all, are they such a great obstacle to their preservation. If they do not have hairy skin, they have no need of it in warm countries, and in cold countries they soon know how to appropriate the skins of beasts they have overcome. If they have only two feet to run with, they have two arms to provide for their defense and their needs. Perhaps their children walk late and with difficulty, but mothers carry them with ease: an advantage lacking in other species in which the mother, being pursued, finds herself forced to abandon her young or to regulate her speed by theirs.* Finally, unless we suppose those singular and fortuitous combinations of circumstances of which I shall speak hereafter and which could very well never happen, it is clear in any case that the first man who made himself clothing or a dwelling, in doing so gave himself things that were hardly necessary, since he had done without them until then and since it is hard to see why he could not endure, as a grown man, a kind of life he had endured from his infancy.

Alone, idle, and always near danger, savage man must like to sleep, and be a light sleeper like animals which, thinking little, sleep so to speak all the time they do not think. His self-preservation being almost his only care, his best-trained faculties must be those having as principal object attack and defense, either to subjugate his prey or to save himself from being the prey of

---

*There may be a few exceptions to this: for example, that animal of the Province of Nicaragua which resembles a fox, has feet like a man's hands, and according to Corréal has a pouch under the stomach where the mother puts her young when she is obliged to flee. This is doubtless the same animal that is called *tlaquatzin* in Mexico, to the female of which Laët ascribes a similar pouch for the same use.

another animal. On the contrary, the organs that are perfected only by softness and sensuality must remain in a state of crudeness which excludes any kind of delicacy in him; and his senses being divided in this regard, he will have extremely crude touch and taste, and sight, hearing, and smell of the greatest subtlety. Such is the animal state in general; and according to reports of travelers, such also is that of most savage peoples. Thus one must not be surprised that the Hottentots of the Cape of Good Hope sight vessels on the high sea with their naked eyes as far away as do the Dutch with spyglasses; nor that American savages could smell Spaniards on the trail as the best dogs could have done; nor that all these barbarous nations endure their nakedness without discomfort, sharpen their taste by means of peppers, and drink European liquors like water.

I have to this point considered only physical man; let us now try to look at him from the metaphysical and moral side.

In every animal I see only an ingenious machine to which nature has given senses in order to revitalize itself and guarantee itself, to a certain point, from all that tends to destroy or upset it. I perceive precisely the same things in the human machine, with the difference that nature alone does everything in the operations of a beast, whereas man contributes to his operations by being a free agent. The former chooses or rejects by instinct and the latter by an act of freedom, so that a beast cannot deviate from the rule that is prescribed to it even when it would be advantageous for it to do so, and a man deviates from it often to his detriment. Thus a pigeon would die of hunger near a basin filled with the best meats, and a cat upon heaps of fruits or grain, although each could very well nourish itself on the food it disdains if it made up its mind to try some. Thus dissolute men abandon themselves to excesses which cause them fever and death, because the mind depraves the senses and because the will still speaks when nature is silent.

Every animal has ideas, since it has senses; it even combines its ideas up to a certain point, and in this regard man differs from a beast only in degree. Some philosophers have even suggested that there is more difference between a given man and another than between a given man and a given beast.[26] Therefore it is not so much understanding which constitutes the distinction of man among the animals as it is his being a free agent. Nature commands every animal, and the beast obeys. Man feels the same impetus, but he realizes that he is free to acquiesce or resist; and it is above all in the consciousness of this freedom that the spirituality of his soul is shown. For physics explains in some way the mechanism of the senses and the formation of ideas; but in the power of willing, or rather of choosing, and in the sentiment of this power are found only purely spiritual acts about which the laws of mechanics explain nothing.

But if the difficulties surrounding all these questions should leave some room for dispute on this difference between man and animal, there is another very specific quality that distinguishes them and about which there can be no dispute: the faculty of self-perfection, a faculty which, with the aid of circumstances, successively develops all the others, and resides among us as much in the species as in the individual. By contrast an animal is at the end of a few months what it will be all its life; and its species is at the end of a thousand years what it was the first year of that thousand. Why is man alone subject to becoming imbecile? Is it not that he thereby returns to his primitive state; and that —while the beast, which has acquired nothing and which has, moreover, nothing to lose, always retains its instinct—man, losing again by old age or other accidents all that his *perfectibility* had made him acquire, thus falls back lower than the beast itself? It would be sad for us to be forced to agree that this distinctive and almost unlimited faculty is the source of all man's misfortunes; that it is this faculty which, by dint of time, draws him out of that original condition in which he would pass tranquil and innocent days; that it is this faculty which, bringing to flower over the centuries his enlightenment and his errors, his vices and his virtues, in the long run makes him the tyrant of himself and of nature (*i*). It would be horrible to be obliged to praise as a beneficent being the one who first suggested to the inhabitant of the banks of the Orinoco the use of those pieces of wood which he binds on the temples of his children, and which assure them at least a part of their imbecility and original happiness.

Savage man, by nature committed to instinct alone, or rather compensated for the instinct he perhaps lacks by faculties capable of substituting for it at first, and then of raising him far above nature, will therefore begin with purely animal functions (*j*). To perceive and feel will be his first state, which he will have in common with all animals. To will and not will, to desire and fear will be the first and almost the only operations of his soul until new circumstances cause new developments in it.

Whatever the moralists may say about it, human

understanding owes much to the passions, which by common agreement also owe much to it. It is by their activity that our reason is perfected; we seek to know only because we desire to have pleasure; and it is impossible to conceive why one who had neither desires nor fears would go to the trouble of reasoning. The passions in turn derive their origin from our needs, and their progress from our knowledge. For one can desire or fear things only through the ideas one can have of them or by the simple impulsion of nature; and savage man, deprived of every kind of enlightenment, feels only the passions of this last kind. His desires do not exceed his physical needs (k), the only goods he knows in the universe are nourishment, a female, and repose; the only evils he fears are pain and hunger. I say pain and not death because an animal will never know what it is to die; and knowledge of death and its terrors is one of the first acquisitions that man has made in moving away from the animal condition.

It would be easy for me, were it necessary, to support this sentiment by facts and to demonstrate that in all nations of the world progress of the mind has been precisely proportioned to the needs that peoples had received from nature or to those to which circumstances had subjected them, and consequently to the passions which inclined them to provide for those needs. I would show the arts coming into existence in Egypt and spreading with the flooding of the Nile. I would follow their progress among the Greeks, where they were seen to spring up, grow, and rise to the heavens among the sands and rocks of Attica though they could not take root on the fertile banks of the Eurotas.[27] I would note that, in general, the peoples of the North are more industrious than those of the South because they can less afford not to be, as if nature thereby wanted to equalize things by giving to minds the fertility it refuses the earth.

But without having recourse to the uncertain testimonies of history, who does not see that everything seems to remove savage man from the temptation and means of ceasing to be savage? His imagination suggests nothing to him; his heart asks nothing of him. His modest needs are so easily found at hand, and he is so far from the degree of knowledge necessary for desiring to acquire greater knowledge, that he can have neither foresight nor curiosity. The spectacle of nature becomes indifferent to him by dint of becoming familiar. There is always the same order, there are always the same revolutions; he does not have the mind to wonder at the greatest marvels; and one must not seek in him the philosophy that man needs in order to know how to observe once what he has seen every day. His soul, agitated by nothing, is given over to the sole sentiment of its present existence without any idea of the future, however near it may be, and his projects, as limited as his views, barely extend to the end of the day. Such is, even today, the degree of foresight of the Carib: in the morning he sells his bed of cotton and in the evening he comes weeping to buy it back, for want of having foreseen that he would need it for the coming night.

The more one meditates on this subject, the more the distance from pure sensations to the simplest knowledge increases in our eyes; and it is impossible to conceive how a man, by his strength alone, without the aid of communication and without the stimulus of necessity, could have bridged so great a gap. How many centuries perhaps elapsed before men were capable of seeing another fire than that from heaven? How many different risks did they have to run to learn the most common uses of that element? How many times did they let it die out before they had acquired the art of reproducing it? And how many times, perhaps, did each of these secrets die with the ones who had discovered it? What shall we say of agriculture, an art which demands so much labor and foresight, which depends on so many other arts, which very clearly is practicable only in a society that has at least been started, and which does not serve so much to bring from the earth foods it would easily provide without agriculture as to force from it those preferences most to our taste? But let us suppose that men had multiplied so greatly that the natural productions no longer sufficed to nourish them: a supposition which, it may be added in passing, would show a great advantage for the human species in that way of life. Let us suppose that without forges and workshops, the implements for farming had fallen from heaven into the hands of the savages; that these men had conquered the mortal hatred they all have for continuous labor; that they had learned to foresee their needs so long in advance; that they had guessed how land must be cultivated, grains sown, and trees planted; that they had discovered the art of grinding wheat and fermenting grapes—all things they would have had to be taught by the gods, as it is impossible to imagine how they could have learned them by themselves. After that, what man would be insane enough to torment himself cultivating a field that will be plundered by the first comer, whether man or beast, for whom the crop is suitable? And how could each man resolve to spend his life in hard labor, when the more he will need its reward, the more certain he will be of not reaping it? In a word, how could this situation incline men to cultivate the earth as long as it is not divided among them: that is to say, as long as the state of nature is not annihilated?

Should we want to suppose a savage man as skillful in the art of thinking as our philosophers make him; should we, following their example, make him a philosopher himself, discovering alone the most sublime truths and making for himself, by chains of very abstract reasoning, maxims of justice and reason drawn from love of order in general or from the known will of his creator; in a word, should we suppose his mind to have as much intelligence and enlightenment as he must and is in fact found to have dullness and stupidity, what utility would the species draw from all this metaphysics, which could not be communicated and which would perish with the individual who would have invented it? What progress could the human race make, scattered in the woods among the animals? And to what point could men mutually perfect and enlighten one another, who, having neither fixed domicile nor any need of one another, would perhaps meet hardly twice in their lives, without knowing or talking to each other.

Let us consider how many ideas we owe to the use of speech; how much grammar trains and facilitates the operations of the mind; and let us think of the inconceivable difficulties and the infinite time which the first invention of languages must have cost. Join these reflections to the preceding ones, and we shall judge how many thousands of centuries would have been necessary to develop successively in the human mind the operations of which it was capable.

May I be allowed to consider for an instant the obstacles to the origin of languages. I could be satisfied to cite or repeat here the researches that the Abbé de Condillac has made on this matter, which all fully confirm my sentiment, and which perhaps gave me the first idea of it. But since the way this philosopher resolves the difficulties he himself raises concerning the origin of instituted signs shows that he assumed what I question—namely, a kind of society already established among the inventors of language—I believe, in referring to his reflections, that I ought to add to them my own, in order to present the same difficulties in the way that suits my subject. The first that comes up is to imagine how language could have become necessary; for since men had no communication among themselves nor any need of it, one can conceive neither the necessity of this invention nor its possibility were it not indispensable. I might well say, as many others do, that languages were born in the domestic intercourse of fathers, mothers, and children. But not only would that fail to resolve the objections, it would be committing the error of those who, reasoning about the state of nature, carry over to it ideas taken from society, and always see the family gathered in the same habitation and its members maintaining among themselves a union as intimate and permanent as among us, where so many common interests unite them. Instead, in the primitive state, having neither houses, nor huts, nor property of any kind, everyone took up his lodging by chance and often for only one night. Males and females united fortuitously, depending on encounter, occasion, and desire, without speech being a very necessary interpreter of the things they had to say to each other; they left each other with the same ease (*l*). The mother nursed her children at first for her own need; then, habit having endeared them to her, she nourished them afterward for their need. As soon as they had the strength to seek their food, they did not delay in leaving the mother herself; and as there was practically no other way to find one another again than not to lose sight of each other, they were soon at a point of not even recognizing one another. Note also that the child having all his needs to explain and consequently more things to say to the mother than the mother to the child, it is the child who must make the greatest efforts of invention, and that the language he uses must be in great part his own work, which multiplies languages as many times as there are individuals to speak them. A wandering and vagabond life contributes further to this, since it does not give any idiom the time to gain consistency. For to say that the mother teaches the child the words he ought to use to ask her for a particular thing shows well how one teaches already formed languages, but it does not teach us how they are formed.

Let us suppose this first difficulty conquered; let us skip over for a moment the immense distance there must have been between the pure state of nature and the need for languages; and let us seek, assuming them to be necessary (*m*), how they could begin to be established. New difficulty, worse still than the preceding one. For if men needed speech in order to learn to think, they had even greater need of knowing how to think in order to discover the art of speech; and even should we understand how the sounds of the voice were taken for the conventional interpreters of our ideas, it would still remain to be seen what could have been the specific interpreters of this convention for ideas that, having no perceptible object, could be indicated neither by gesture nor by voice. So that one can hardly form tenable conjectures about the birth of this art of communicating thoughts and establishing intercourse between minds: a sublime art which is now very far from its origin, but which the philosopher still sees at so prodigious a distance from its perfection that no man is bold enough to guarantee it will ever achieve it, even should the revolutions time necessarily brings be suspended in its favor, should prejudices quit the academies or be silent before them, and should they be able attend to that thorny matter for whole centuries without interruption.[28]

Man's first language, the most universal, most energetic, and only language he needed before it was necessary to persuade assembled men, is the cry of nature. As this cry was elicited only by a kind of instinct in pressing emergencies, to beg for help in great dangers, or for relief in violent ills, it was not of much use in the ordinary course of life, where more moderate sentiments prevail. When the ideas of men began to spread and multiply, and when closer communication was established among them, they sought more numerous signs and a more extensive language; they multiplied the inflections of the voice, and joined to it gestures which are more expressive by their nature, and whose meaning is less dependent on prior determination. They therefore expressed visible and mobile objects by gestures, and audible ones by imitative sounds. But because gesture indicates hardly anything except present or easily described objects and visible actions; because its usage is not universal since darkness or the interposition of a body render it useless; and since it requires attention rather than stimulates it, men finally thought to substitute articulations of the voice which, without having the same relation to certain ideas, are better suited to represent all ideas as instituted signs: a substitution which cannot be made except by a common consent, and in a way rather difficult to practice for men whose crude organs as yet had no training, and even more difficult to conceive in itself, since that unanimous agreement must have had a motive, and since speech seems to have been highly necessary in order to establish the use of speech.

One must conclude that the first words men used had in their mind a much broader meaning than do those used in already formed languages; and being ignorant of the division of discourse into its constituent parts, they at first gave each word the meaning of a whole sentence. When they began to distinguish subject from attribute and verb from noun, which was no small effort of genius, substantives were at first only so many proper nouns; the present infinitive was the sole tense of verbs; and the notion of adjectives must have developed only with great difficulty, because every adjective is an abstract word and abstractions are difficult and not very natural operations.

Every object received at first a particular name, without regard to genus and species, which these first institutors were incapable of distinguishing; and all individual things appeared to their minds in isolation as they are in the panorama of nature. If one oak was called A another was called B, for the first idea one infers from two things is that they are not the same; and often much time is needed to observe what they have in common. So that the more limited the knowledge, the more extensive the dictionary. The obstacle of all this nomenclature could not easily be removed, for in order to organize beings under common and generic denominations, it was necessary to know their properties and differences. Observations and definitions were necessary—that is to say, much more natural history and metaphysics than the men of those times could have had.

Besides, general ideas can come into the mind only with the aid of words, and the understanding grasps them only through propositions. That is one of the reasons why animals can neither formulate such ideas nor ever acquire the perfectibility which depends on them. When a monkey goes without hesitating from one nut to another, is it thought that he has a general idea of this kind of fruit and that he compares its archetype to these two individuals? Doubtless not; but the sight of one of these nuts recalls to his memory the sensations he received from the other, and his eyes, modified in a certain way, announce to his taste the modification it is going to receive. Every general idea is purely intellectual; if imagination is in the least involved, the idea immediately becomes particular. Try to draw for yourself the image of a tree in general, you will never succeed in doing it; despite yourself it must be seen small or large, sparse or leafy, light or dark; and if it were up to you to see in it only what is found in every tree, this image would no longer re-

semble a tree. Purely abstract beings are seen in the
same way, or are conceived only through discourse.
The definition of the triangle alone gives you the true
idea of it: as soon as you imagine one in your mind,
it is a given triangle and not another, and you cannot
avoid making its lines perceptible or its plane colored.
It is therefore necessary to state propositions, hence to
speak, in order to have general ideas; for as soon as the
imagination stops, the mind goes no further without
the help of discourse. If, then, the first inventors could
give names only to ideas they already had, it follows
that the first substantives could never have been anything but proper nouns.

But when, by means that I cannot conceive, our new
grammarians began to extend their ideas and to general-
ize their words, the ignorance of the inventors must
have subjected this method to very narrow limitations;
and just as at first they had overly multiplied the names
of individual things for want of knowing the genera
and species, they then made too few species and genera
for want of having considered beings by all their differences. To extend the divisions far enough would have
required more experience and enlightenment than they
could have had, and more research and labor than they
wanted to put into it. Now if even today new species
are daily discovered that had eluded all our observations until now, think how many species must have
been hidden from men who judged things only on first
sight! As for primary classes and the most general notions, it is superfluous to add that they still must have
escaped them. How, for example, would they have
imagined or understood the words matter, mind, substance, mode, figure, movement, since our philosophers,

who have used them for such a long time, have much trouble understanding them themselves; and since, the ideas attached to these words being purely metaphysical, they found no model of them in nature?

I stop with these first steps, and beg my judges to suspend their reading here to consider, concerning the invention of physical substantives alone—that is to say, concerning the easiest part of the language to discover —how far language still has to go to express all the thoughts of men, assume a consistent form, be capable of being spoken in public, and influence society. I beg them to reflect upon how much time and knowledge were necessary to discover numbers (n), abstract words, aorists, and all the tenses of verbs, particles, syntax, the linking of propositions, reasoning, and the forming of all the logic of discourse. For myself, frightened by the multiplying difficulties, and convinced of the almost demonstrated impossibility that languages could have arisen and been established by purely human means, I leave to whomever would undertake it the discussion of the following difficult problem: Which was most necessary, previously formed society for the institution of languages; or previously invented languages for the establishment of society?

Whatever these origins may be, from the little care taken by nature to bring men together through mutual needs and to facilitate their use of speech, one at least sees how little it prepared their sociability, and how little it contributed to everything men have done to establish social bonds. In fact, it is impossible to imagine why, in that primitive state, a man would sooner have need of another man than a monkey or a wolf of its fellow creature; nor, supposing this need, what motive could induce the other to provide for it, nor even, in this last case, how they could agree between them on the conditions. I know we are repeatedly told that nothing would have been so miserable as man in that state; and if it is true, as I believe I have proved, that only after many centuries could man have had the desire and opportunity to leave that state, it would be a fault to find with nature and not with him who would have been so constituted by nature. But if I understand properly this term *miserable,* it is a word that has no meaning or only signifies a painful privation and the suffering of the body or soul. Now I would really like someone to explain to me what type of misery there can be for a free being whose heart is at peace and whose body is healthy? I ask which, civil or natural life, is most liable to become unbearable to those who enjoy it? We see around us practically no people who do not complain of their existence, even many who deprive themselves of it insofar as they have the capacity; and the combination of divine and human laws hardly suffices to stop this disorder. I ask if anyone has ever heard it said that a savage in freedom even dreamed of complaining about life and killing himself. Let it then be judged with less pride on which side true misery lies. Nothing, on the contrary, would have been so miserable as savage man dazzled by enlightenment, tormented by passions, and reasoning about a state different from his own. It was by a very wise providence that his potential faculties were to develop only with the opportunities to exercise them, so that they were neither superfluous and burdensome to him beforehand, nor tardy and useless when needed. He had, in instinct alone, everything necessary

for him to live in the state of nature: he has, in a cultivated reason, only what is necessary for him to live in
society.

It seems at first that men in that state, not having
among themselves any kind of moral relationship or
known duties, could be neither good nor evil, and had
neither vices nor virtues: unless, taking these words in
a physical sense, one calls vices in the individual the
qualities that can harm his own preservation, and virtues those that can contribute to it; in which case, it
would be necessary to call the most virtuous the one
who least resists the simple impulses of nature. But
without departing from the ordinary meaning, it is appropriate to suspend the judgment we could make of
such a situation and to beware of our prejudices, until
one has examined with scale in hand whether there are
more virtues than vices among civilized men; or
whether their virtues are more advantageous than their
vices are deadly; or whether the progress of their knowledge is a sufficient compensation for the harms they do
one another as they learn of the good they ought to do;
or whether all things considered, they would not be
in a happier situation having neither harm to fear nor
good to hope for from anyone, rather than subjecting
themselves to a universal dependence and obliging
themselves to receive everything from those who do not
obligate themselves to give them anything.

Above all, let us not conclude with Hobbes that because man has no idea of goodness he is naturally evil;
that he is vicious because he does not know virtue; that
he always refuses his fellow-men services he does not
believe he owes them; nor that, by virtue of the right
he reasonably claims to things he needs, he foolishly

imagines himself to be the sole proprietor of the whole universe. Hobbes saw very clearly the defect of all modern definitions of natural right; but the consequences he draws from his own definition show that he takes it in a sense which is no less false. Reasoning upon the principles he establishes, this author ought to have said that since the state of nature is that in which care of our self-preservation is the least prejudicial to the self-preservation of others, that state was consequently the best suited to peace and the most appropriate for the human race. He says precisely the opposite, because of having improperly included in the savage man's care of self-preservation the need to satisfy a multitude of passions which are the product of society and which have made laws necessary.[29] The evil man, he says, is a robust child. It remains to be seen whether savage man is a robust child. Should we grant this to him, what would he conclude from it? That if, when he is robust, this man were as dependent on others as when he is weak, there is no kind of excess to which he would not be inclined: that he would beat his mother when she would be too slow in giving him her breast; that he would strangle one of his young brothers when he would be inconvenienced by him; that he would bite another's leg when he was hit or annoyed by it. But to be robust and to be dependent are two contradictory suppositions in the state of nature. Man is weak when he is dependent, and he is emancipated before he is robust. Hobbes did not see that the same cause that prevents savages from using their reason, as our jurists claim, prevents them at the same time from abusing their faculties, as he himself claims. Thus one could say that savages are not evil precisely because they do not know what it is to be good; for it is neither the growth of enlightenment nor the restraint of law, but the calm of passions and the ignorance of vice which prevent them from doing evil: *Tanto plus in illis proficit vitiorum ignoratio, quam in his cognitio virtutis.*[30] There is, besides, another principle which Hobbes did not notice, and which—having been given to man in order to soften, under certain circumstances, the ferocity of his vanity or the desire for self-preservation before the birth of vanity (o)[31]—tempers the ardor he has for his own well-being by an innate repugnance to see his fellow-man suffer. I do not believe I have any contradiction to fear in granting man the sole natural virtue that the most excessive detractor of human virtues was forced to recognize.[32] I speak of pity, a disposition that is appropriate to beings as weak and subject to as many ills as we are; a virtue all the more universal and useful to man because it precedes in him the use of all reflection; and so natural that even beasts sometimes give perceptible signs of it. Without speaking of the tenderness of mothers for their young and of the perils they brave to guard them, one observes daily the repugnance of horses to trample a living body underfoot. An animal does not pass near a dead animal of its species without uneasiness. There are even some animals that give them a kind of sepulcher; and the sad lowing of cattle entering a slaughterhouse announces the impression they receive from the horrible sight that strikes them. One sees with pleasure the author of the *Fable of the Bees*, forced to recognize man as a compassionate and sensitive being, departing from his cold and subtle style in the example he gives in order to offer us the pathetic

image of an imprisoned man who sees outside a wild
beast tearing a child from his mother's breast, breaking
his weak limbs in its murderous teeth, and ripping
apart with its claws the palpitating entrails of this child.
What horrible agitation must be felt by this witness of
an event in which he takes no personal interest! What
anguish must he suffer at this sight, unable to bring
help to the fainting mother or to the dying child.[33]

Such is the pure movement of nature prior to all
reflection. Such is the force of natural pity, which the
most depraved morals still have difficulty destroying,
since daily in our theaters one sees, moved and crying
for the troubles of an unfortunate person, a man who,
if he were in the tyrant's place, would aggravate his
enemy's torments even more—like bloodthirsty Sulla,
so sensitive to ills he had not caused,[34] or like Alexander
of Pherae, who did not dare attend the performance of
any tragedy lest he be seen moaning with Andromache
and Priam, whereas he listened without emotion to the
cries of so many citizens murdered daily on his orders.[35]

> Mollissima corda
> Humano generi dare se natura fatetur,
> Quæ lacrimas dedit.[36]

Mandeville sensed very well that even with all their
ethics men would never have been anything but
monsters if nature had not given them pity in support
of reason; but he did not see that from this quality
alone flow all the social virtues he wants to question
in men. In fact, what are generosity, clemency, humanity, if not pity applied to the weak, to the guilty,
or to the human species in general? Benevolence and
even friendship are, rightly understood, the products

of a constant pity fixed on a particular object: for is desiring that someone not suffer anything but desiring that he be happy? Even should it be true that commiseration is only a sentiment that puts us in the position of him who suffers—a sentiment that is obscure and strong in savage man, developed but weak in civilized man—what would this idea matter to the truth of what I say, except to give it more force? In fact, commiseration will be all the more energetic as the observing animal identifies himself more intimately with the suffering animal. Now it is evident that this identification must have been infinitely closer in the state of nature than in the state of reasoning. Reason engenders vanity and reflection fortifies it; reason turns man back upon himself, it separates him from all that bothers and afflicts him. Philosophy isolates him; because of it he says in secret, at the sight of a suffering man: Perish if you will, I am safe. No longer can anything except dangers to the entire society trouble the tranquil sleep of the philosopher and tear him from his bed. His fellow-man can be murdered with impunity right under his window; he has only to put his hands over his ears and argue with himself a bit to prevent nature, which revolts within him, from identifying him with the man who is being assassinated. Savage man does not have this admirable talent, and for want of wisdom and reason he is always seen heedlessly yielding to the first sentiment of humanity. In riots or street fights the populace assembles, the prudent man moves away; it is the rabble, the marketwomen, who separate the combatants and prevent honest people from murdering each other.

It is very certain, therefore, that pity is a natural

sentiment which, moderating in each individual the activity of love of oneself, contributes to the mutual preservation of the entire species. It carries us without reflection to the aid of those whom we see suffer; in the state of nature, it takes the place of laws, morals, and virtue, with the advantage that no one is tempted to disobey its gentle voice; it will dissuade every robust savage from robbing a weak child or an infirm old man of his hard-won subsistence if he himself hopes to be able to find his own elsewhere. Instead of that sublime maxim of reasoned justice, *Do unto others as you would have them do unto you,* it inspires all men with this other maxim of natural goodness, much less perfect but perhaps more useful than the preceding one: *Do what is good for you with the least possible harm to others.* In a word, it is in this natural sentiment, rather than in subtle arguments, that we must seek the cause of the repugnance every man would feel in doing evil, even independently of the maxims of education. Although it may behoove Socrates and minds of his stamp to acquire virtue through reason, the human race would have perished long ago if its preservation had depended only on the reasonings of its members.

With such inactive passions and such a salutary restraint, men—more untamed than evil, and more attentive to protecting themselves from harm they could receive than tempted to harm others—were not subject to very dangerous quarrels. Since they had no kind of commerce among themselves; since they consequently knew neither vanity, nor consideration, nor esteem, nor contempt; since they did not have the slightest notion of thine and mine, nor any true idea of justice; since they regarded the violences they might suffer as harm easy to redress and not as an insult which must be punished, and since they did not even dream of vengeance, except perhaps mechanically and on the spot, like the dog that bites the stone thrown at him, their disputes would rarely have had bloody consequences had there been no more sensitive subject than food. But I see a more dangerous subject left for me to discuss.

Among the passions that agitate the heart of man, there is an ardent, impetuous one that makes one sex necessary to the other; a terrible passion which braves all dangers, overcomes all obstacles, and which, in its fury, seems fitted to destroy the human race it is destined to preserve. What would become of men, tormented by this unrestrained and brutal rage, without chastity, without modesty, daily fighting over their loves at the price of their blood?

It must first be agreed that the more violent the passions, the more necessary laws are to contain them. But besides the fact that the disorders and crimes these passions cause every day among us show well enough the inadequacy of laws in this regard, it would still be good to examine whether these disorders did not arise with the laws themselves; for then, even should they be capable of repressing these disorders, the very least that ought to be required of the laws is to stop an evil which would not exist without them.

Let us begin by distinguishing between the moral and the physical in the sentiment of love. The physical is that general desire which inclines one sex to unite with the other. The moral is that which determines this desire and fixes it exclusively on a single object, or which at least gives it a greater degree of energy for this preferred object. Now it is easy to see that the moral element of love is an artificial sentiment born of the usage of society, and extolled with much skill and care by women in order to establish their ascendancy and make dominant the sex that ought to obey. This sentiment, founded on certain notions of merit or beauty that a savage is not capable of having, and on comparisons he is not capable of making, must be almost null for him. For as his mind could not form abstract ideas of regularity and proportion, so his heart is not susceptible to the sentiments of admiration and love that, even without its being noticed, arise from the application of these ideas. He heeds solely the temperament he received from nature, and not the taste he has not been able to acquire; any woman is good for him.

Limited solely to that which is physical in love, and fortunate enough to be ignorant of those preferences that irritate its sentiment and augment its difficulties, men must feel the ardors of their temperament less frequently and less vividly, and consequently have fewer and less cruel disputes among themselves. Imagination, which causes so much havoc among us, does not speak to savage hearts. Everyone peaceably waits for the impulsion of nature, yields to it without choice with more pleasure than frenzy; and the need satisfied, all desire is extinguished.

It is therefore incontestable that love itself, like all the other passions, has acquired only in society that impetuous ardor which so often makes it fatal for men; and it is all the more ridiculous to portray savages continually murdering each other to satisfy their brutality as this opinion is directly contrary to experience, and as the Caribs, that of all existing peoples which until now has departed least from the state of nature, are precisely the most peaceful in their loves and the least subject to jealousy, even though they live in a burning hot climate, which always seems to give greater activity to these passions.

Regarding inferences that one could draw, in some species of animals, from the fights of males which bloody our farmyards in all seasons or which make our forests resound with their cries in Spring as they contend for a female, it is necessary to begin by excluding all species in which nature has manifestly established, in the relative power of the sexes, other relations than among us: thus cockfights do not provide an inference for the human species. In species where the proportion is better observed, these fights can have for causes only the scarcity of females with reference to the number of males, or the exclusive intervals during which the female constantly refuses to let the male approach her, which amounts to the first cause; for if each female tolerates the male during only two months of the year, in this respect it is the same as if the number of females were reduced by five-sixths. Now neither of these two cases is applicable to the human species, in which the number of females generally surpasses the number of males, and in which it has never been observed that, even among savages, females, like those of other species, have times of heat and exclusion. Moreover, among some of these animals, since the entire species enters a state of heat at the same time, there comes a terrible moment of general ardor, tumult, disorder, and fighting: a moment that does not take place in the human species, in which love is never periodic. Therefore one cannot conclude from the fights of certain animals for the possession of females that the same thing would happen to man in the state of nature. And even if one could draw that conclusion, as these dissensions do not destroy the other species, one must consider at least that they would not be more fatal to ours; and it is very apparent that they would cause still less havoc in the state of nature than they do in society, particularly in countries where, morals still counting for something, the jealousy of lovers and the vengeance of husbands are a daily cause of duels, murders, and worse things; where the obligation to eternal fidelity serves only to create adulterers; and where even the laws of continence and honor necessarily spread debauchery and multiply abortions.

Let us conclude that wandering in the forests, without industry, without speech, without domicile, without war and without liaisons, with no need of his fellowmen, likewise with no desire to harm them, perhaps never even recognizing anyone individually, savage man, subject to few passions and self-sufficient, had only the sentiments and intellect suited to that state; he felt only his true needs, saw only what he believed he had an interest to see; and his intelligence made no more progress than his vanity. If by chance he made some discovery, he was all the less able to communicate it because he did not recognize even his children. Art perished with the inventor. There was neither education nor progress; the generations multiplied uselessly; and everyone always starting from the same point, centuries passed in all the crudeness of the first ages; the species was already old, and man remained ever a child.

If I have spent so much time on the supposition of

this primitive condition, it is because, having ancient errors and inveterate prejudices to destroy, I thought I ought to dig down to the root and show, in the panorama of the true state of nature, how far even natural inequality is from having as much reality and influence in that state as our writers claim.

In fact, it is easy to see that, among the differences that distinguish men, some pass for natural that are uniquely the work of habit and the various types of life men adopt in society. Thus a robust or delicate temperament, and the strength or weakness that depend on it, often come more from the harsh or effeminate way in which one has been raised than from the primitive constitution of bodies. The same is true of strength of mind; and not only does education establish a difference between cultivated minds and those which are not, but it augments the difference among the former in proportion to their culture; for should a giant and a dwarf walk on the same road, every step they both take will give fresh advantage to the giant. Now if one compares the prodigious diversity of educations and types of life that prevails in the different orders of the civil state with the simplicity and uniformity of animal and savage life, in which all nourish themselves on the same foods, live in the same manner, and do exactly the same things, it will be understood how much less the difference between one man and another must be in the state of nature than in society, and how much natural inequality must increase in the human species through instituted inequality.

But even should nature assign as many preferences in the distribution of its gifts as is claimed, what advantage would the most favored draw from them to the prejudice of others in a state of things which permitted almost no sort of relationship among them? Where there is no love, of what use is beauty? What is the use of wit for people who do not speak, and ruse for those who have no dealings? I hear it always repeated that the stronger will oppress the weak. But let someone explain to me what is meant by this word oppression. Some will dominate by violence, the others will groan, enslaved to all their whims. That is precisely what I observe among us; but I do not see how that could be said of savage men, to whom one would even have much trouble explaining what servitude and domination are. A man might well seize the fruits another has gathered, the game he has killed, the cave that served as his shelter; but how will he ever succeed in making himself obeyed? And what can be the chains of dependence among men who possess nothing? If someone chases me from one tree, I am at liberty to go to another; if someone torments me in one place, who will prevent me from going elsewhere? Is there a man whose strength is sufficiently superior to mine and who is, in addition, depraved enough, lazy enough, and wild enough to force me to provide for his subsistence while he remains idle? He must resolve not to lose sight of me for a single moment and to keep me very carefully tied up during his sleep, for fear that I should escape or kill him—that is to say, he is obliged to expose himself voluntarily to much greater trouble than he wants to avoid and gives to me. After all that, should his vigilance relax for a moment, should an unforseen noise make him turn his head, I take twenty steps in the forest, my chains are broken, and he never in his life sees me again.

Without uselessly prolonging these details, everyone must see that, since the bonds of servitude are formed only from the mutual dependence of men and the reciprocal needs that unite them, it is impossible to enslave a man without first putting him in the position of being unable to do without another; a situation which, as it did not exist in the state of nature, leaves each man there free of the yoke, and renders vain the law of the stronger.

After having proved that inequality is barely perceptible in the state of nature, and that its influence there is almost null, it remains for me to show its origin and progress in the successive developments of the human mind. After having shown that *perfectibility*, social virtues, and the other faculties that natural man had received in potentiality could never develop by themselves, that in order to develop they needed the chance combination of several foreign causes which might never have arisen and without which he would have remained eternally in his primitive condition, it remains for me to consider and bring together the different accidents that were able to perfect human reason while deteriorating the species, make a being evil while making him sociable, and from such a distant origin finally bring man and the world to the point where we see them.

I admit that as the events I have to describe could have happened in several ways, I can make a choice only by conjectures. But besides the fact that these conjectures become reasons when they are the most probable that one can draw from the nature of things, and the sole means that one can have to discover the truth, the conclusions I want to deduce from mine will not thereby be conjectural, since, on the principles I have established, one could not conceive of any other system that would not provide me with the same results, and from which I could not draw the same conclusions.

This will excuse me from expanding my reflections concerning the way in which the lapse of time compensates for the slight probability of events; concerning the surprising power of very trivial causes when they act without interruption; concerning the impossibility, on the one hand, for one to destroy certain hypotheses, although on the other one cannot give them the degree of certainty of facts; concerning how, when two facts given as real are to be connected by a series of intermediate facts which are unknown or considered as such, it is up to history, when it exists, to present the facts that connect them; while it is up to philosophy, when history is lacking, to determine similar facts that might connect them; finally, concerning how, with reference to events, similarity reduces the facts to a much smaller number of different classes than is imagined. It is enough for me to offer these objects to the consideration of my judges; it is enough for me to have arranged it so that vulgar readers would have no need to consider them.

SECOND PART

The first person who, having fenced off a plot of ground, took it into his head to say *this is mine* and found people simple enough to believe him, was the true founder of civil society. What crimes, wars, murders, what miseries and horrors would the human race have been spared by someone who, uprooting the stakes or filling in the ditch, had shouted to his fellow-men: Beware of listening to this impostor; you are lost if you forget that the fruits belong to all and the earth to no one! But it is very likely that by then things had already come to the point where they could no longer remain as they were. For this idea of property, depending on many prior ideas which could only have arisen successively, was not conceived all at once in the human mind. It was necessary to make much progress, to acquire much industry and enlightenment, and to transmit and augment them from age to age, before arriving at this last stage of the state of nature. Therefore let us start further back in time and attempt to assemble from a single point of view this slow succession of events and knowledge in their most natural order.

Man's first sentiment was that of his existence, his first care that of his preservation. The products of the earth furnished him with all the necessary help; instinct led him to make use of them. Hunger and other appetites making him experience by turns various manners of existing, there was one appetite that invited him to perpetuate his species; and this blind inclination, devoid of any sentiment of the heart, produced only a purely animal act. This need satisfied, the two sexes no longer recognized each other, and even the child no longer meant anything to his mother as soon as he could do without her.

Such was the condition of nascent man; such was the life of an animal limited at first to pure sensations and scarcely profiting from the gifts nature offered him, far from dreaming of wresting anything from it. But difficulties soon arose; it was necessary to learn to conquer them. The height of trees, which prevented him from reaching their fruits, the competition of animals that sought to nourish themselves with these fruits, the ferocity of those animals that wanted to take his very life, all obliged him to apply himself to bodily exercises. It was necessary to become agile, fleet in running, vigorous in combat. Natural arms, which are branches of trees and stones, were soon discovered at hand. He learned to surmount nature's obstacles, combat other animals when necessary, fight for his subsistence even with men, or make up for what had to be yielded to the stronger.

In proportion as the human race spread, difficulties multiplied along with men. Differences of soil, climate, and season could force them to admit differences in their ways of life. Barren years, long and hard winters, and scorching summers which consume everything required of them new industry. Along the sea and rivers they invented the fishing line and hook, and became fishermen and eaters of fish. In forests they made bows and arrows, and became hunters and warriors. In cold countries they covered themselves with the skins of beasts they had killed. Lightning, a volcano, or some happy accident introduced them to fire, a new resource against the rigor of winter. They learned to preserve this element, then to reproduce it, and finally to prepare with it meats they previously devoured raw.

This repeated utilization of various beings in relation to himself, and of some beings in relation to others, must naturally have engendered in man's mind perceptions of certain relations. Those relationships that we express by the words large, small, strong, weak, fast, slow, fearful, bold, and other similar ideas, compared when necessary and almost without thinking about it, finally produced in him some sort of reflection, or rather a mechanical prudence that indicated to him the precautions most necessary for his safety.

The new enlightenment that resulted from this development increased his superiority over the other animals by making him aware of his superiority. He practiced setting traps for them; he tricked them in a thousand ways; and although several surpassed him in strength at fighting, or in speed at running, of those which might serve him or hurt him he became with time the master of the former, and the scourge of the latter. Thus the first glance he directed upon himself produced in him the first stirring of pride; thus, as yet scarcely knowing how to distinguish ranks, and considering himself in the first rank as a species, he prepared himself from afar to claim first rank as an individual.

Although his fellow-men were not for him what they are for us, and although he scarcely had more intercourse with them than with other animals, they were not forgotten in his observations. The conformities that time could make him perceive among them, his female, and himself led him to judge of those which he did not perceive; and seeing that they all behaved as he would have done under similar circumstances, he concluded that their way of thinking and feeling conformed entirely to his own. And this important truth, well established in his mind, made him follow, by a premonition as sure as dialectic and more prompt, the best rules of conduct that it was suitable to observe toward them for his advantage and safety.

Taught by experience that love of well-being is the sole motive of human actions, he found himself able to distinguish the rare occasions when common interest should make him count on the assistance of his fellow-men, and those even rarer occasions when competition should make him distrust them. In the first case he united with them in a herd; or at most by some kind of free association that obligated no one and lasted only as long as the passing need that had formed it. In the second case, everyone sought to obtain his own advantage, either by naked force if he believed he could, or by cleverness and cunning if he felt himself to be the weaker.

That is how men could imperceptibly acquire some crude idea of mutual engagements and of the advantages of fulfilling them, but only insofar as present and perceptible interest could require; for foresight meant nothing to them, and far from being concerned about a distant future, they did not even think of the next day. Was it a matter of catching a deer, everyone clearly felt that for this purpose he ought faithfully to keep his post; but if a hare happened to pass within reach of one of them, there can be no doubt that he pursued it without scruple, and that having obtained his prey, he cared very little about having caused his companions to miss theirs.

It is easy to understand that such intercourse did not require a language much more refined than that of crows or monkeys, which group together in approximately the same way. For a long time inarticulate cries, many gestures, and some imitative noises must have composed the universal language; by joining to this in each country a few articulated and conventional sounds—the institution of which, as I have already said, is not too easy to explain—there were particular languages, but crude imperfect ones, approximately like those which various savage nations still have today.

I cover multitudes of centuries like a flash, forced by the time that elapses, the abundance of things I have to say, and the almost imperceptible progress of the beginnings; for the more slowly events followed upon one another, the more quickly they can be described.

These first advances finally put man in a position to make more rapid ones. The more the mind was enlightened, the more industry was perfected. Soon, ceasing to fall asleep under the first tree or to withdraw into caves, they discovered some kinds of hatchets of hard, sharp stones, which served to cut wood, scoop out earth, and make huts from branches they later decided to coat with clay and mud. This was the epoch of a first revolution, which produced the establishment and differentiation of families, and which introduced a sort of property—from which perhaps many quarrels and fights already arose. However, as the stronger were probably the first to make themselves lodgings they felt capable of defending, it is to be presumed that the weak found it quicker and safer to imitate them than to try to dislodge them; and as for those who already had huts, each man must seldom have sought to appropriate his neighbor's, less because it did not belong to him than because it was of no use to him, and because he could not seize it without exposing himself to a lively fight with the family occupying it.

The first developments of the heart were the effect of a new situation, which united husbands and wives, fathers and children in a common habitation. The habit of living together gave rise to the sweetest sentiments known to men: conjugal love and paternal love. Each family became a little society all the better united because reciprocal affection and freedom were its only bonds; and it was then that the first difference was established in the way of life of the two sexes, which until this time had had but one. Women became more sedentary and grew accustomed to tend the hut and the children, while the man went to seek their common subsistence. The two sexes also began, by their slightly softer life, to lose something of their ferocity and vigor. But if each one separately became less suited to combat savage beasts, on the contrary it was easier to assemble in order to resist them jointly.

In this new state, with a simple and solitary life, very limited needs, and the implements they had invented to provide for them, since men enjoyed very great leisure, they used it to procure many kinds of commodities unknown to their fathers; and that was the first yoke they imposed on themselves without thinking about it, and the first source of the evils they prepared for their descendants. For, besides their continuing thus to soften body and mind, as these commodities had lost almost all their pleasantness through habit, and as they had at the same time degenerated into true needs, being deprived of them became much more cruel than possessing them was sweet; and people were unhappy to lose them without being happy to possess them.

At this point one catches a slightly better glimpse of how the use of speech was established or perfected imperceptibly in the bosom of each family; and one can conjecture further how particular causes could have spread language and accelerated its progress by making it more necessary. Great floods or earthquakes surrounded inhabited cantons with water or precipices; revolutions of the globe detached and broke up portions of the continent into islands. One conceives that among men thus brought together and forced to live together, a common idiom must have been formed sooner than among those who wandered freely in the forests on solid ground. Thus it is very possible that after their first attempts at navigation, islanders brought the use of speech to us; and it is at least very probable that society and languages came into being on islands and were perfected there before they were known on the continent.

Everything begins to change its appearance. Men who until this time wandered in the woods, having adopted a more fixed settlement, slowly come together, unite into different bands, and finally form in each country a particular nation, unified by customs and character, not by regulations and laws but by the same kind of life and foods and by the common influence of climate. A permanent proximity cannot fail to engender at length some contact between different families. Young people of different sexes live in neighboring huts; the passing intercourse demanded by nature soon leads to another kind no less sweet and more permanent through mutual frequentation. People grow accustomed to consider different objects and to make comparisons; imperceptibly they acquire ideas of merit and beauty which produce sentiments of preference. By dint of seeing one another, they can no longer do without seeing one another again. A tender and gentle sentiment is gradually introduced into the soul and at the least obstacle becomes an impetuous fury. Jealousy awakens with love; discord triumphs, and the gentlest of the passions receives sacrifices of human blood.

In proportion as ideas and sentiments follow upon one another and as mind and heart are trained, the human race continues to be tamed, contacts spread, and bonds are tightened. People grew accustomed to assembling in front of the huts or around a large tree; song and dance, true children of love and leisure, became the amusement or rather the occupation of idle and assembled men and women. Each one began to look at the others and to want to be looked at himself, and public esteem had a value. The one who sang or danced the best, the handsomest, the strongest, the most adroit, or the most eloquent became the most highly considered; and that was the first step toward inequality and, at the same time, toward vice. From these first preferences were born on one hand vanity and contempt, on the other shame and envy; and the fermentation caused by these new leavens eventually produced compounds fatal to happiness and innocence.

As soon as men had begun to appreciate one another, and the idea of consideration was formed in their minds, each one claimed a right to it, and it was no longer possible to be disrespectful toward anyone with impunity. From this came the first duties of civility, even among savages; and from this any voluntary wrong became an outrage, because along with the harm that resulted from the injury, the offended man saw in it contempt for his person which was often more unbearable than the harm itself. Thus, everyone punishing the contempt shown him by another in a manner proportionate to the importance he accorded himself, vengeances became terrible, and men bloodthirsty and

cruel. This is precisely the point reached by most of
the savage peoples known to us, and it is for want of
having sufficiently distinguished between ideas and
noticed how far these peoples already were from the
first state of nature that many have hastened to conclude that man is naturally cruel, and that he needs
civilization in order to make him gentler. On the contrary, nothing is so gentle as man in his primitive state
when, placed by nature at equal distances from the
stupidity of brutes and the fatal enlightenment of civil
man, and limited equally by instinct and reason to
protecting himself from the harm that threatens him,
he is restrained by natural pity from harming anyone
himself, and nothing leads him to do so even after he
has received harm. For, according to the axiom of the
wise Locke, *where there is no property, there is no
injury.*[37]

But it must be noted that the beginnings of society
and the relations already established among men required in them qualities different from those they
derived from their primitive constitution; that, morality
beginning to be introduced into human actions, and
each man, prior to laws, being sole judge and avenger
of the offenses he had received, the goodness suitable
for the pure state of nature was no longer that which
suited nascent society; that it was necessary for punishments to become more severe as the occasions for offense
became more frequent; and that it was up to the terror
of revenge to take the place of the restraint of laws.
Thus although men had come to have less endurance
and although natural pity had already undergone some
alteration, this period of the development of human
faculties, maintaining a golden mean between the indo-

lence of the primitive state and the petulant activity of our vanity, must have been the happiest and most durable epoch. The more one thinks about it, the more one finds that this state was the least subject to revolutions, the best for man (p), and that he must have come out of it only by some fatal accident, which for the common good ought never to have happened. The example of savages, who have almost all been found at this point, seems to confirm that the human race was made to remain in it always; that this state is the veritable prime of the world; and that all subsequent progress has been in appearance so many steps toward the perfection of the individual, and in fact toward the decrepitude of the species.

As long as men were content with their rustic huts, as long as they were limited to sewing their clothing of skins with thorns or fish bones, adorning themselves with feathers and shells, painting their bodies with various colors, perfecting or embellishing their bows and arrows, carving with sharp stones a few fishing canoes or a few crude musical instruments; in a word, as long as they applied themselves only to tasks that a single person could do and to arts that did not require the cooperation of several hands, they lived free, healthy, good, and happy insofar as they could be according to their nature, and they continued to enjoy among themselves the sweetness of independent intercourse. But from the moment one man needed the help of another, as soon as they observed that it was useful for a single person to have provisions for two, equality disappeared, property was introduced, labor became necessary; and vast forests were changed into smiling fields which had to be watered with the sweat of men, and in which slavery and misery were soon seen to germinate and grow with the crops.

Metallurgy and agriculture were the two arts whose invention produced this great revolution. For the poet it is gold and silver, but for the philosopher it is iron and wheat which have civilized men and ruined the human race.[38] Accordingly, both of these were unknown to the savages of America, who therefore have always remained savage; other peoples even seem to have remained barbarous as long as they practiced one of these arts without the other. And perhaps one of the best reasons why Europe has been, if not earlier, at least more constantly and better civilized than the other parts of the world is that it is at the same time the most abundant in iron and the most fertile in wheat. It is very difficult to guess how men came to know and use iron; for it is not credible that by themselves they thought of drawing the raw material from the mine and giving it the necessary preparations to fuse it before they knew what would result. From another point of view, it is even harder to attribute this discovery to some accidental fire, because mines are formed only in arid spots, stripped of both trees and plants; so that one would say that nature had taken precautions to hide this deadly secret from us. There only remains, therefore, the extraordinary circumstance of some volcano which, by throwing up metallic materials in fusion, would have given observers the idea of imitating this operation of nature. Even so, it is necessary to suppose in them much courage and foresight to undertake such difficult labor and to envisage so far in advance the advantages they could gain from it: all of which hardly suits minds that are not already more trained than theirs must have been.

With regard to agriculture, its principle was known long before its practice was established, and it is hardly possible that men, constantly occupied with obtaining their subsistence from trees and plants, did not rather promptly have an idea of the ways used by nature to grow plants. But their industry probably turned in that direction only very late, either because trees, which along with hunting and fishing provided their food, did not have need of their care; or for want of knowing how to use wheat; or for want of implements to cultivate it; or for want of foresight concerning future need; or, finally, for want of means to prevent others from appropriating the fruit of their labor. Once they became industrious, it is credible that, with sharp stones and pointed sticks, they began by cultivating a few vegetables or roots around their huts long before they knew how to prepare wheat and had the implements necessary for large-scale cultivation. Besides, to devote oneself to that occupation and seed the land, one must be resolved to lose something at first in order to gain a great deal later: a precaution very far from the turn of mind of savage man, who, as I have said, has great difficulty thinking in the morning of his needs for the evening.

The invention of the other arts was therefore necessary to force the human race to apply itself to that of agriculture. As soon as some men were needed to smelt and forge iron, other men were needed to feed them. The more the number of workers was multiplied, the fewer hands were engaged in furnishing the common subsistence, without there being fewer mouths to consume it; and since some needed foodstuffs in exchange for their iron, the others finally found the secret of using iron in order to multiply foodstuffs. From this arose husbandry and agriculture on the one hand, and on the other the art of working metals and multiplying their uses.

From the cultivation of land, its division necessarily followed; and from property once recognized, the first rules of justice. For in order to give everyone what is his, it is necessary that everyone can have something; moreover, as men began to look to the future and as they all saw themselves with some goods to lose, there was not one of them who did not have to fear reprisals against himself for wrongs he might do to another. This origin is all the more natural as it is impossible to conceive of the idea of property arising from anything except manual labor; because one can not see what man can add, other than his own labor, in order to appropriate things he has not made. It is labor alone which, giving the cultivator a right to the product of the land he has tilled, gives him a right to the soil as a consequence, at least until the harvest, and thus from year to year; which, creating continuous possession, is easily transformed into property. When the ancients, says Grotius, gave Ceres the epithet of legislatrix, and gave the name of Thesmaphories to a festival celebrated in her honor, they thereby made it clear that the division of lands produced a new kind of right: that is, the right of property, different from the one which results from natural law.[39]

Things in this state could have remained equal if talents had been equal, and if, for example, the use of iron and the consumption of foodstuffs had always been exactly balanced. But this proportion, which nothing maintained, was soon broken; the stronger did more work; the cleverer turned his to better advantage; the more ingenious found ways to shorten his labor; the farmer had greater need of iron or the blacksmith greater need of wheat; and working equally, the onꜰ earned a great deal while the other barely had enough to live. Thus does natural inequality imperceptibly manifest itself along with contrived inequality; and thus do the differences among men, developed by those of circumstances, become more perceptible, more permanent in their effects, and begin to have a proportionate influence over the fate of individuals.

Things having reached this point, it is easy to imagine the rest. I shall not stop to describe the successive invention of the other arts, the progress of languages, the testing and use of talents, the inequality of fortunes, the use or abuse of wealth, nor all the details that follow these, and that everyone can easily fill in. I shall simply limit myself to casting a glance at the human race placed in this new order of things.

Behold all our faculties developed, memory and imagination in play, vanity aroused, reason rendered active, and the mind having almost reached the limit of the perfection of which it is susceptible. Behold all the natural qualities put into action, the rank and fate of each man established, not only upon the quantity of goods and the power to serve or harm, but also upon the mind, beauty, strength, or skill, upon merit or talents. And these qualities being the only ones which could attract consideration, it was soon necessary to have them or affect them; for one's own advantage, it was necessary to appear to be other than what one in fact was. To be and to seem to be became two altogether different things; and from this distinction came conspicuous ostentation, deceptive cunning, and all the vices that follow from them. From another point of view, having formerly been free and independent, behold man, due to a multitude of new needs, subjected so to speak to all of nature and especially to his fellowmen, whose slave he becomes in a sense even in becoming their master; rich, he needs their services; poor, he needs their help; and mediocrity cannot enable him to do without them.[40] He must therefore incessantly seek to interest them in his fate, and to make them find their own profit, in fact or in appearance, in working for his. This makes him deceitful and sly with some, imperious and harsh with others, and makes it necessary for him to abuse all those whom he needs when he cannot make them fear him and does not find his interest in serving them usefully. Finally, consuming ambition, the fervor to raise one's relative fortune less out of true need than in order to place oneself above others, inspires in all men a base inclination to harm each other, a secret jealousy all the more dangerous because, in order to strike its blow in greater safety, it often assumes the mask of benevolence: in a word, competition and rivalry on one hand, opposition of interest on the other; and always the hidden desire to profit at the expense of others. All these evils are the first effect of property and the inseparable consequence of nascent inequality.

Before representative signs of wealth had been invented, it could hardly consist of anything except land and livestock, the only real goods men can possess. Now when inheritances had increased in number and extent to the point of covering the entire earth and of all bordering on each other, some of them could no longer be enlarged except at the expense of others; and the supernumeraries, whom weakness or indolence had prevented from acquiring an inheritance in their turn, having become poor without having lost anything— because while everything around them changed they alone had not changed at all—were obliged to receive or steal their subsistence from the hand of the rich; and from that began to arise, according to the diverse characters of the rich and the poor, domination and servitude or violence and rapine. The rich, for their part, had scarcely known the pleasure of domination when they soon disdained all others, and using their old slaves to subdue new ones, they thought only of subjugating and enslaving their neighbors: like those famished wolves which, having once tasted human flesh, refuse all other food and thenceforth want only to devour men.

Thus, as the most powerful or most miserable made of their force or their needs a sort of right to the goods of others, equivalent according to them to the right of property, the destruction of equality was followed by the most frightful disorder; thus the usurpations of the rich, the brigandage of the poor, the unbridled passions of all, stifling natural pity and the as yet weak voice of justice, made man avaricious, ambitious, and evil. Between the right of the stronger and the right of the first occupant there arose a perpetual conflict which ended only in fights and murders (q). Nascent society gave way to the most horrible state of war: the human race, debased and desolated, no longer able to turn back or renounce the unhappy acquisitions it had made, and working only toward its shame by abusing the faculties that honor it, brought itself to the brink of its ruin.

Attonitus novitate mali, divesque, miserque,
Effugere optat opes, et quæ modo voverat, odit.[41]

It is not possible that men should not at last have
reflected upon such a miserable situation and upon
the calamities overwhelming them. The rich above
all must have soon felt how disadvantageous to them
was a perpetual war in which they alone paid all the
costs, and in which the risk of life was common to all
while the risk of goods was theirs alone. Moreover,
whatever pretext they might give for their usurpations,
they were well aware that these were established only
on a precarious and abusive right, and that having
been acquired only by force, force could take them
away without their having grounds for complaint. Even
those enriched by industry alone could hardly base
their property upon better titles. In vain might they say:
But I built this wall; I earned this field by my labor.
Who gave you its dimensions, they might be answered,
and by virtue of what do you presume to be paid at
our expense for work we did not impose on you? Do you
not know that a multitude of your brethren die or
suffer from need of what you have in excess, and that
you needed express and unanimous consent of the
human race to appropriate for yourself anything from
common subsistence that exceeded your own? Destitute
of valid reasons to justify himself and of sufficient
forces to defend himself; easily crushing an individual,
but himself crushed by groups of bandits; alone against
all, and unable because of mutual jealousies to unite
with his equals against enemies united by the common
hope of plunder, the rich, pressed by necessity, finally
conceived the most deliberate project that ever entered

the human mind. It was to use in his favor the very forces of those who attacked him, to make his defenders out of his adversaries, inspire them with other maxims, and give them other institutions which were as favorable to him as natural right was adverse.

To this end, after having shown his neighbors the horror of a situation that made them all take up arms against one another, that made their possessions as burdensome as their needs, and in which no one found security in either poverty or wealth, he easily invented specious reasons to lead them to his goal. "Let us unite," he says to them, "to protect the weak from oppression, restrain the ambitious, and secure for everyone the possession of what belongs to him. Let us institute regulations of justice and peace to which all are obliged to conform, which make an exception of no one, and which compensate in some way for the caprices of fortune by equally subjecting the powerful and the weak to mutual duties. In a word, instead of turning our forces against ourselves, let us gather them into one supreme power which governs us according to wise laws, protects and defends all the members of the association, repulses common enemies, and maintains us in an eternal concord."

Far less than the equivalent of this discourse was necessary to win over crude, easily seduced men, who in addition had too many disputes to straighten out among themselves to be able to do without arbiters, and too much avarice and ambition to be able to do without masters for long. All ran to meet their chains thinking they secured their freedom, for although they had enough reason to feel the advantages of a political establishment, they did not have enough experience to forsee its dangers. Those most capable of anticipating the abuses were precisely those who counted on profiting from them; and even the wise saw the necessity of resolving to sacrifice one part of their freedom for the preservation of the other, just as a wounded man has his arm cut off to save the rest of his body.

Such was, or must have been, the origin of society and laws, which gave new fetters to the weak and new forces to the rich (r), destroyed natural freedom for all time, established forever the law of property and inequality, changed a clever usurpation into an irrevocable right, and for the profit of a few ambitious men henceforth subjected the whole human race to work, servitude, and misery. It is easily seen how the establishment of a single society made that of all the others indispensable, and how, to stand up to the united forces, it was necessary to unite in turn. Societies, multiplying or spreading rapidly, soon covered the entire surface of the earth; and it was no longer possible to find a single corner in the universe where one could free oneself from the yoke and withdraw one's head from the sword, often ill-guided, that every man saw perpetually hanging over his head. Civil right having thus become the common rule of citizens, the law of nature no longer operated except between the various societies, where, under the name law of nations, it was tempered by some tacit conventions in order to make intercourse possible and to take the place of natural commiseration which, losing between one society and another nearly all the force it had between one man and another, no longer dwells in any but a few great cosmopolitan souls, who surmount the imaginary barriers that separate peoples and who, following the example of the sovereign Being who created them, include the whole human race in their benevolence.[42]

The bodies politic, thus remaining in the state of nature with relation to each other, soon experienced the inconveniences that had forced individuals to leave it; and among these great bodies that state became even more fatal than it had previously been among the individuals of whom they were composed. Hence arose the national wars, battles, murders, and reprisals which make nature tremble and shock reason, and all those horrible prejudices which rank the honor of shedding human blood among the virtues. The most decent men learned to consider it one of their duties to murder their fellow-men; at length men were seen to massacre each other by the thousands without knowing why; more murders were committed on a single day of fighting and more horrors in the capture of a single city than were committed in the state of nature during whole centuries over the entire face of the earth. Such are the first effects one glimpses of the division of the human race into different societies. Let us return to their institution.

I know that many have attributed other origins to political societies, such as conquests by the more powerful, or union of the weak; and the choice among these causes is indifferent to what I want to establish. However, the one I have just presented appears to me the most natural for the following reasons. 1. In the first case, the right of conquest, as it is not a right, could not have founded any other, since the conqueror and the conquered peoples always remain toward each other in a state of war, unless the nation, given back its complete freedom, should voluntarily choose its conqueror as its chief. Until then, whatever capitulations may have been made, as they have been founded only upon violence and are consequently null by that very fact, following this hypothesis there can be neither true society nor body politic, nor any other law than that of the stronger. 2. These words *strong* and *weak* are equivocal in the second case; for, in the interval between the establishment of the right of property or of the first occupant and that of political governments, the meaning of these terms is better expressed by the terms *poor* and *rich*, since before the laws a man did not, in fact, have any other means of subjecting his equals than by attacking their goods or by giving them some of his. 3. The poor having nothing to lose except their freedom, it would have been great folly for them to give away voluntarily the sole good remaining to them, gaining nothing in the exchange; on the contrary, the rich being so to speak vulnerable in every part of their goods, it was much easier to harm them; they consequently had more precautions to take in order to protect themselves from harm; and finally it is reasonable to believe that a thing was invented by those to whom it is useful rather than by those whom it wrongs.

Nascent government did not have a constant and regular form. The lack of philosophy and experience allowed only present inconveniences to be perceived, and men thought of remedying others only as they presented themselves. Despite all the labors of the wisest legislators, the political state remained ever imperfect because it was almost the work of chance, and because, as it began badly, time in discovering faults and suggesting remedies could never repair the vices of the constitution. People incessantly mended, whereas it would have been necessary to begin by clearing the area and setting aside all the old materials, as Lycurgus did in Sparta, in order to raise a good edifice afterward. At first society consisted only of some general conventions which all individuals pledged to observe, and regarding which the community became the guarantor for each individual. Experience had to show how weak such a constitution was, and how easy it was for lawbreakers to avoid conviction or punishment for faults of which the public alone was to be witness and judge; the law had to be evaded in a thousand ways; inconveniences and disorders had to multiply continually in order that men finally thought of confiding to private persons the dangerous trust of public authority, and committed to magistrates the care of enforcing obedience to the deliberations of the people. For to say that the chiefs were chosen before the confederation was created and that the ministers of laws existed before the laws themselves is a supposition that does not permit of serious debate.[43]

It would be no more reasonable to believe that at first peoples threw themselves into the arms of an absolute master without conditions and for all time, and that the first means of providing for the common security imagined by proud and unconquered men was to rush into slavery. In fact, why did they give themselves superiors if not to defend themselves against oppression, and to protect their goods, their freedoms, and their lives, which are, so to speak, the constituent elements of their being? Now in relations between one man and another, as the worst that can happen to one is to see himself at the discretion of the other, would it not have been contrary to good sense to begin by surrendering into the hands of a chief the only things they needed his help to preserve? What equivalent could he have offered them for the concession of so fine a right? And had he dared to require it under pretext of defending them, would he not promptly have received the answer of the allegory: What more will the enemy do to us? It is therefore incontestable, and it is the fundamental maxim of all political right, that peoples have given themselves chiefs to defend their freedom and not to enslave themselves. *If we have a prince,* said Pliny to Trajan, *it is so that he may preserve us from having a master.*[44]

Our politicians make the same sophisms about love of freedom that our philosophers have made about the state of nature; by the things they see they make judgments about very different things which they have not seen. And they attribute to men a natural inclination to servitude due to the patience with which those who are before their eyes bear their servitude, without thinking that it is the same for freedom as for innocence and virtue—their value is felt only as long as one enjoys them oneself, and the taste for them is lost as soon as one has lost them. I know the delights of your country, said Brasidas to a satrap who compared the life of Sparta to that of Persepolis; but you cannot know the pleasures of mine.[45]

As an untamed steed bristles his mane, paws the earth with his hoof, and breaks away impetuously at the very approach of the bit, whereas a trained horse patiently endures whip and spur, barbarous man does not bend his head for the yoke that civilized man wears without a murmur, and he prefers the most turbulent freedom to tranquil subjection. Therefore it is not by

the degradation of enslaved peoples that man's natural
dispositions for or against servitude must be judged,
but by the marvels done by all free peoples to guard
themselves from oppression. I know that the former do
nothing but boast incessantly of the peace and repose
they enjoy in their chains, and that *miserrimam servitutem pacem appellant.*[46] But when I see the others
sacrifice pleasures, repose, wealth, power, and life itself
for the preservation of this sole good which is so disdained by those who have lost it; when I see animals
born free and despising captivity break their heads
against the bars of their prison; when I see multitudes
of entirely naked savages scorn European voluptuous-
ness and endure hunger, fire, the sword, and death to
preserve only their independence, I feel that it does
not behoove slaves to reason about freedom.

Regarding paternal authority, from which many have
derived absolute government and all society, without
having recourse to the contrary proofs of Locke and
Sidney,[47] it suffices to note that nothing in the world
is farther from the ferocious spirit of despotism than
the gentleness of that authority which looks more to
the advantage of the one who obeys than to the utility
of the one who commands; that by the law of nature,
the father is master of the child only as long as his help
is necessary for him; that beyond this stage they become equals, and the son, perfectly independent of the
father, then owes him only respect and not obedience;
for gratitude is certainly a duty which must be rendered,
but not a right which one can require. Instead of saying
that civil society is derived from paternal power, it
should be said on the contrary that it is from civil
society that this power draws its principle force. An

individual was not recognized as the father of many until they remained assembled around him. The goods of the father, of which he is truly the master, are the bonds which keep his children dependent on him, and he can give them a share of his inheritance only in proportion as they shall have properly deserved it from him by continual deference to his wishes. Now subjects, far from having some similar favor to expect from their despot, since they and all they possess belong to him as personal belongings—or at least he claims this to be the case—are reduced to receiving as a favor what he leaves them of their own goods. He renders justice when he plunders them; he renders grace when he lets them live.

Continuing thus to test the facts by right, one would find no more solidity than truth in the voluntary establishment of tyranny; and it would be difficult to show the validity of a contract that would obligate only one of the parties, where all would be given to one side and nothing to the other, and that would only damage the one who binds himself. This odious system is very far from being, even today, that of wise and good monarchs, and especially of the Kings of France, as may be seen in various parts of their edicts and particularly in the following passage of a famous writing, published in 1667 in the name and by orders of Louis XIV: *Let it not be said therefore that the sovereign is not subject to the laws of his State, since the contrary proposition is a truth of the law of nations, which flattery has sometimes attacked, but which good princes have always defended as a tutelary divinity of their States. How much more legitimate is it to say, with wise Plato, that the perfect felicity of a kingdom is that a prince be obeyed by his subjects, that the prince obey the law, and that the law be right and always directed to the public good.*[48] I shall not stop to inquire whether, freedom being the most noble of man's faculties, it is not degrading one's nature, putting oneself on the level of beasts enslaved by instinct, even offending the author of one's being, to renounce without reservation the most precious of all his gifts and subject ourselves to committing all the crimes he forbids us in order to please a ferocious or insane master; nor whether this sublime workman must be more irritated to see his finest work destroyed than to see it dishonored. I shall neglect, if one wishes, the authority of Barbeyrac, who clearly declares, following Locke, that no one can sell his freedom to the point of subjecting himself to an arbitrary power which treats him according to its fancy: *Because,* he adds, *that would be selling one's own life, of which one is not the master.*[49] I shall only ask by what right those who have not been afraid of so greatly debasing themselves have been able to subject their posterity to the same ignominy, and to renounce for it goods which do not depend on their liberality and without which life itself is burdensome to all who are worthy of it.

Pufendorf says that just as one transfers his goods to another by conventions and contracts, one can also divest himself of his freedom in favor of someone else.[50] That, it seems to me, is very bad reasoning: for, first, the goods I alienate become something altogether foreign to me, the abuse of which is indifferent to me; but it matters to me that my freedom is not abused, and I cannot, without making myself guilty of the evil I shall be forced to do, risk becoming the instrument of

crime. Moreover, as the right of property is only conventional and of human institution, every man can
dispose at will of what he possesses. But it is not the
same for the essential gifts of nature, such as life and
freedom, which everyone is permitted to enjoy and of
which it is at least doubtful that one has the right to
divest himself: by giving up the one, one degrades his
being, by giving up the other one destroys it insofar
as he can; and as no temporal goods can compensate
for the one or the other, it would offend both nature
and reason to renounce them whatever the price. But
if one could alienate his freedom like his goods, there
would be a very great difference for children, who enjoy
the father's goods only by transmission of his right;
whereas since freedom is a gift they receive from nature
by being men, their parents did not have any right to
divest them of it. So that just as to establish slavery
violence had to be done to nature, nature had to be
changed to perpetuate this right; and the jurists, who
have gravely pronounced that the child of a slave would
be born a slave, have decided in other terms that a man
would not be born a man.

It therefore appears certain to me not only that
governments did not begin by arbitrary power, which
is only their corruption and extreme limit, and which
finally brings them back to the sole law of the strongest
for which they were originally the remedy; but also
that even if they had begun thus, this power, being
by its nature illegitimate, could not have served as a
foundation for the rights of society, nor consequently
for instituted inequality.

Without entering at present into the researches yet
to be undertaken concerning the nature of the funda-

mental compact of all government, I limit myself, in following common opinion, to consider here the establishment of the body politic as a true contract between the people and the chiefs it chooses for itself: a contract by which the two parties obligate themselves to observe laws that are stipulated in it and that form the bonds of their union.[51] The people having, on the subject of social relations, united all their wills into a single one, all the articles on which this will is explicit become so many fundamental laws obligating all members of the State without exception, and one of these laws regulates the choice and power of magistrates charged with watching over the execution of the others. This power extends to everything that can maintain the constitution, without going so far as to change it. To it are joined honors which make the laws and their ministers respectable and, for the latter personally, prerogatives which compensate them for the difficult labors that good administration requires. The magistrate, for his part, obligates himself to use the power confided in him only according to the intention of the constituents, to maintain each one in the peaceable enjoyment of what belongs to him, and to prefer on all occasions the public utility to his own interest.

Before experience had shown or knowledge of the human heart had made men foresee the inevitable abuses of such a constitution, it must have appeared all the better because those who were charged with watching over its preservation were themselves the most interested in it. For the magistracy and its rights being established only upon the fundamental laws, should they be destroyed the magistrates would immediately cease to be legitimate, the people would no longer be bound to obey them; and as it would not have been the magistrate but the law which had constituted the essence of the State, everyone would return by right to his natural freedom.[52]

With the slightest attentive reflection, this would be confirmed by additional reasons, and by the nature of the contract one would see that it could not be irrevocable: for if there were no superior power which could guarantee the fidelity of the contracting parties nor force them to fulfill their reciprocal engagements, the parties would remain sole judges of their own case, and each of them would always have the right to renounce the contract as soon as he should find that the other breaks its conditions or as soon as the conditions should cease to suit him. It is on this principle that it seems the right to abdicate can be founded. Now to consider, as we are doing, only what is of human institution, if the magistrate who has all the power in his hands and who appropriates for himself all the advantages of the contract, nonetheless had the right to renounce his authority, there is all the more reason that the people, who pay for all the faults of the chiefs, ought to have the right to renounce their dependence. But the frightful dissensions, the infinite disorders that this dangerous power would necessarily entail demonstrate more than anything else how much human governments needed a basis more solid than reason alone, and how necessary it was for public repose that divine will intervened to give sovereign authority a sacred and inviolable character which took from the subjects the fatal right of disposing of it. If religion had accomplished only this good for men, it would be enough to oblige them all to cherish and adopt it, even with its abuses, since it spares even more blood than fanaticism causes to be shed.[53] But let us follow the thread of our hypothesis.

The various forms of governments derive their origin from the greater or lesser differences to be found among individuals at the moment of institution. Was one man eminent in power, virtue, wealth, or credit, he alone was elected magistrate, and the State became monarchical. If several approximately equal among themselves prevailed over all others, they were elected jointly and there was an aristocracy. Those whose fortune or talents were less disproportionate, and who were the least removed from the state of nature, kept the supreme administration in common and formed a democracy. Time verified which of these forms was the most advantageous for men. Some remained solely subject to laws, the others soon obeyed masters. The citizens wanted to keep their freedom; the subjects thought only of taking it away from their neighbors, since it was unbearable that others should enjoy a good which they themselves no longer enjoyed. In a word, on one side were wealth and conquests, and on the other happiness and virtue.

In these various governments, all magistracies were at first elective; and when wealth did not prevail, preference was accorded to merit, which gives a natural ascendancy, and to age, which gives experience in affairs and composure in deliberations. The elders of the Hebrews, the gerontes of Sparta, the senate of Rome, and the very etymology of our word *seigneur*[54] show how much old age was respected in former times. The more elections fell to men advanced in age, the more frequent elections became and the more their difficulties were felt. Intrigues were introduced, factions were formed, parties grew bitter, civil wars broke out; finally the blood of citizens was sacrificed to the so-called happiness of the State, and men were at the point of falling back into the anarchy of earlier times. The ambition of leading personages profited from these circumstances to perpetuate their posts in their families; the people, already accustomed to dependence, repose, and the conveniences of life, and already incapable of breaking their chains, consented to let their servitude increase in order to assure their tranquillity. Thus the chiefs, having become hereditary, grew accustomed to consider their magistracy as a family possession, to regard themselves as proprietors of the State, of which they were at first only the officers, to call their fellow citizens their slaves, count them like cattle in the number of things that belonged to them, and call themselves equals of the gods and kings of kings.

If we follow the progress of inequality in these different revolutions, we shall find that the establishment of the law and of the right of property was the first stage, the institution of the magistracy the second, and the third and last was the changing of legitimate power into arbitrary power. So that the status of rich and poor was authorized by the first epoch, that of powerful and weak by the second, and by the third that of master and slave, which is the last degree of inequality and the limit to which all the others finally lead, until new revolutions dissolve the government altogether or bring it closer to its legitimate institution.

To understand the necessity of this progress, one must consider less the motives for the establishment of the body politic than the form it takes in its execution and the inconveniences it brings along with it: for the vices that make social institutions necessary are the same ones that make their abuse inevitable. And as—excepting Sparta alone, where the law attended principally to the education of children and where Lycurgus established morals which almost allowed him to dispense with adding laws—laws, in general less strong than passions, contain men without changing them, it would be easy to prove that any government that, without being corrupted or altered, always worked exactly according to the ends of its institution, would have been instituted unnecessarily, and that a country where no one eluded the laws and abused the magistracy would need neither magistracy nor laws.

Political distinctions necessarily bring about civil distinctions. The growing inequality between the people and its chiefs soon makes itself felt among individuals, where it is modified in a thousand ways according to passions, talents, and events. The magistrate cannot usurp illegitimate power without creating some protégés to whom he is forced to yield some part of it. Besides, citizens let themselves be oppressed only insofar as they are carried away by blind ambition; and looking more below than above them, domination becomes dearer to them than independence, and they consent to wear chains in order to give them to others in turn.[55] It is very difficult to reduce to obedience one who does not seek command; and the most adroit politician would never succeed in subjecting men who wanted only to be free. But inequality spreads without difficulty among ambitious and cowardly souls, always ready to run the risks of fortune, and to dominate or serve almost indifferently, according to whether it becomes favorable or adverse to them. Thus there must have come a time when the eyes of the people were so bewitched that their leaders had only to say to the smallest of men: Be great, you and all your line; immediately he appeared great to everyone as well as in his own eyes, and his descendants were exalted even more in proportion to their distance from him. The more remote and uncertain the cause, the more the effect augmented; the more idlers one could count in a family, the more illustrious it became.

If this were the place to go into details, I would easily explain how, even without the involvement of government, inequality of credit and authority becomes inevitable between individuals (s) as soon as, united in the same society, they are forced to make comparisons between themselves and to take into account differences they find in the continual use they have to make of one another. These differences are of several kinds; but in general wealth, nobility or rank, power, and personal merit being the principal distinctions by which one is measured in society, I would prove that the agreement or conflict of these various forces is the surest indication of a well- or ill-constituted state. I would show that of these four types of inequality, as personal qualities are the origin of all the others, wealth is the last to which they are reduced in the end because, being the most immediately useful to well-being and the easiest to communicate, it is easily used to buy all the rest: an observation which can permit a rather exact judgment of the extent to which each people is removed from its primitive institution, and of the distance it has traveled toward the extreme limit of corruption. I would point out how much that universal desire for reputation, honors, and preferences, which devours us all, trains and compares talents and strengths; how much it stimulates and multiplies passions; and making all men competitors, rivals, or rather enemies, how many reverses, successes, and catastrophes of all kinds it causes daily by making so many contenders race the same course. I would show that to this ardor to be talked about, to this furor to distinguish oneself, which nearly always keeps us outside of ourselves, we owe what is best and worst among men, our virtues and our vices, our sciences and our errors, our conquerors and our philosophers—that is to say, a multitude of bad things as against a small number of good ones. Finally, I would prove that if one sees a handful of powerful and rich men at the height of grandeur and fortune, while the crowd grovels in obscurity and misery, it is because the former prize the things they enjoy only insofar as the others are deprived of them; and because, without changing their status, they would cease to be happy if the people ceased to be miserable.

But these details alone would be the subject matter of a considerable work in which one would weigh the advantages and inconveniences of all governments relative to the rights of the state of nature, and where one would unmask all the different faces behind which inequality has appeared until the present and may appear in future centuries, according to the nature of these governments and the revolutions time will necessarily bring about in them. One would see the multitude oppressed within as a consequence of the very precautions it had taken against that which menaced it from without; one would see oppression grow continually, without the oppressed ever being able to know what its limit would be, or what legitimate means would be left them to stop it; one would see the rights of citizens and national freedoms die out little by little, and the protests of the weak treated as seditious murmurs; one would see politics limit to a mercenary portion of the people the honor of defending the common cause; from that one would see arise the necessity of taxes, the discouraged farmer abandoning his field, even during peacetime, and leaving his plough to buckle on the sword; one would see emerge the fatal and bizarre rules of the point of honor; one would see the defenders of the country become, sooner or later, its enemies, incessantly holding the dagger over their fellow-citizens, and there would come a time when one would hear them say to the oppressor of their country:

Pectore si fratris gladium juguloque parentis
Condere me jubeas, gravidæque in viscera partu
Conjugis, invita peragam tamen omnia dextra.[56]

From the extreme inequality of conditions and fortunes, from the diversity of passions and talents, from useless arts, from pernicious arts, from frivolous sciences would come scores of prejudices equally contrary to reason, happiness, and virtue. One would see chiefs foment all that can weaken assembled men by disuniting them; all that can give society an air of apparent concord while spreading a seed of real division; all that can inspire defiance and mutual hatred in different orders through the opposition of their rights and interests, and consequently fortify the power that contains them all.

It is from the bosom of this disorder and these revolutions that despotism, by degrees raising its hideous head and devouring all it had seen to be good and healthy in all parts of the State, would finally succeed in trampling underfoot the laws and the people, and in establishing itself upon the ruins of the Republic. The times that would precede this last change would be times of troubles and calamities, but in the end everything would be engulfed by the monster, and peoples would no longer have chiefs or laws but only tyrants. From that moment also morals and virtue would cease to be in question; for wherever despotism reigns, *cui ex honesto nulla est spes* [57], it tolerates no other master. As soon as it speaks, there is neither probity nor duty to consult, and the blindest obedience is the sole virtue which remains for slaves.

Here is the ultimate stage of inequality, and the extreme point which closes the circle and touches the point from which we started. Here all individuals become equals again because they are nothing; and subjects no longer having any law except the will of the master, nor the master any other rule except his passions, the notions of good and the principles of justice vanish once again. Here everything is brought back to the sole law of the stronger, and consequently to a new state of nature different from the one with which we began, in that the one was the state of nature in its purity, and this last is the fruit of an excess of corruption. Besides, there is so little difference between these two states, and the contract of government is so completely dissolved by despotism, that the despot is master only as long as he is the strongest, and as soon as he can be driven out, he cannot protest against violence. The uprising that ends by strangling or dethroning a sultan is as lawful an act as those by which he disposed, the day before, of the lives and goods of his subjects. Force alone maintained him, force alone overthrows him. Everything thus occurs according to the natural order; and whatever the outcome of these short and frequent revolutions may be, no one can complain of another's injustice, but only of his own imprudence or his misfortune.

In discovering and following thus the forgotten and lost routes that must have led man from the natural state to the civil state; in re-establishing, along with the intermediary positions I have just noted, those that the pressure of time has made me suppress or that imagination has not suggested to me, every attentive reader cannot fail to be struck by the immense space that separates these two states. It is in this slow succession of things that he will see the solution to an infinite number of problems of ethics and politics which the philosophers cannot resolve. He will sense that, the human race of one age not being the human race of another, the reason Diogenes did not find a man was that he sought among his contemporaries the man of a time that no longer existed. Cato, he will say, perished with Rome and freedom because he was out of place in his century; and the greatest of men only astonished the world, which he would have governed five hundred years earlier. In a word, he will explain how the soul and human passions, altering imperceptibly, change their nature so to speak; why our needs and our pleasures change their objects in the long run; why, original man vanishing by degrees, society no longer offers to the eyes of the wise man anything except an assemblage of artificial men and factitious passions which are the work of all these new relations and have no true foundation in nature. What reflection teaches us on this subject, observation confirms perfectly: savage man and civilized man differ so much in the bottom of their

SECOND DISCOURSE / 179

hearts and inclinations that what constitutes the supreme happiness of one would reduce the other to despair. The former breathes only repose and freedom; he wants only to live and remain idle; and even the perfect quietude of the Stoic does not approach his profound indifference for all other objects. On the contrary, the citizen, always active, sweats, agitates himself, torments himself incessantly in order to seek still more laborious occupations; he works to death, he even rushes to it in order to get in condition to live, or renounces life in order to acquire immortality. He pays court to the great whom he hates, and to the rich whom he scorns. He spares nothing in order to obtain the honor of serving them; he proudly boasts of his baseness and their protection; and proud of his slavery, he speaks with disdain of those who do not have the honor of sharing it. What a sight the difficult and envied labors of a European minister are for a Carib! How many cruel deaths would that indolent savage not prefer to the horror of such a life, which often is not even sweetened by the pleasure of doing good. But in order to see the goal of so many cares, the words *power* and *reputation* would have to have a meaning in his mind; he would have to learn that there is a kind of men who set some store by the consideration of the rest of the universe and who know how to be happy and content with themselves on the testimony of others rather than on their own. Such is, in fact, the true cause of all these differences: the savage lives within himself; the sociable man, always outside of himself, knows how to live only in the opinion of others; and it is, so to speak, from their judgment alone that he draws the sentiment of his own existence. It is not part of my subject to show how, from such a disposition, so much indifference for good and evil arises along with such fine discourses on ethics; how, everything being reduced to appearances, every: thing becomes factitious and deceptive: honor, friendship, virtue, and often even vices themselves, about which men finally discover the secret of boasting; how, in a word, always asking others what we are and never daring to question ourselves on this subject, in the midst of so much philosophy, humanity, politeness, and sublime maxims, we have only a deceitful and frivolous exterior, honor without virtue, reason without wisdom, and pleasure without happiness. It is sufficient for me to have proved that this is not the original state of man; and that it is the spirit of society alone, and the inequality it engenders, which thus change and alter all our natural inclinations.

I have tried to set forth the origin and progress of inequality, the establishment and abuse of political societies, insofar as these things can be deduced from the nature of man by the light of reason alone, and independently of the sacred dogmas which give to sovereign authority the sanction of divine right. It follows from this exposition that inequality, being almost null in the state of nature, draws its force and growth from the development of our faculties and the progress of the human mind, and finally becomes stable and legitimate by the establishment of property and laws. It follows, further, that moral inequality, authorized by positive right alone, is contrary to natural right whenever it is not combined in the same proportion with physical inequality: a distinction which sufficiently determines what one ought to think in this regard of the sort of inequality that reigns among all civilized people;

since it is manifestly against the law of nature, in whatever manner it is defined, that a child command an old man, an imbecile lead a wise man, and a handful of men be glutted with superfluities while the starving multitude lacks necessities.[58]

Rousseau's Notes

Page 79 (a) Herodotus relates that after the murder of the false Smerdis, the seven liberators of Persia being assembled to deliberate upon the form of government they would give the State, Otanes was strongly in favor of a Republic: an opinion all the more extraordinary in the mouth of a satrap as, besides the claim he could have to the empire, grandees fear more than death a sort of government that forces them to respect men. Otanes, as may easily be believed, was not heeded; and seeing that they were going to proceed to the election of a monarch, he, who wanted neither to obey nor command, voluntarily yielded his right to the crown to the other competitors, asking as his only compensation that he and his posterity be free and independent. This was granted him.[59] If Herodotus did not inform us of the restriction that was placed on this privilege, it would be necessary to suppose it; otherwise Otanes, not recognizing any sort of law and being accountable to no one, would have been all-powerful in the State and more powerful than the king himself.[60] But there was hardly any likelihood that a man capable of contenting himself with such a privilege, in a case like that, was capable of abusing it. In fact, it cannot be seen that this right ever caused the least trouble in the kingdom, either by wise Otanes or by any of his descendants.[61]

Page 91 (b) From the outset I rely with confidence upon one of those authorities that are respectable for philosophers because they come from a solid and sublime reason, which philosophers alone know how to find and appreciate.

ROUSSEAU'S NOTES / 183

"Whatever interest we may have to know ourselves, I am not sure whether we do not know better everything that is not ourselves. Provided by nature with organs destined uniquely for our preservation, we use them only to receive foreign impressions, we seek only to extend beyond ourselves, and exist outside ourselves. Too busy multiplying the functions of our senses and augmenting the external range of our being, we rarely make use of that internal sense which reduces us to our true dimensions, and which separates from us all that is not part of us. However, it is this sense we must use if we wish to know ourselves; it is the only one by which we can judge ourselves. But how can this sense be made active and given its full range? How can we rid our soul, in which it resides, of all the illusions of our mind? We have lost the habit of using it, it has remained without exercise in the midst of the tumult of our bodily sensations, it has been dried out by the fire of our passions; heart, mind, senses, everything has worked against it." HIST. NAT., T. 4, p. 151, *de la Nat. de l'homme.*[62]

Page 104 (*c*) The changes that a long habit of walking on two feet could have produced in the conformation of man, the relationships still noted between his arms and the forelegs of quadrupeds, and the induction drawn from their way of walking, have given rise to doubts about the way that must have been most natural for us. All children begin by walking on all fours, and need our example and our lessons to learn to stand up. There are even savage nations, such as the Hottentots, who, greatly neglecting their children, let them walk on their hands for so long that they then have great difficulty making them straighten up; the children of the Caribs of the Antilles do the same thing. There are various examples of quadruped men; and among others I could cite that of the child who was found in 1344 near Hesse, where he had been raised by wolves, and who said afterward at the court of Prince Henry that if it had been up to him, he would have preferred to return to them than to live among men. He had so thoroughly adopted the habit of walking like those animals that it was necessary to attach pieces of wood to him that forced him to stand up and keep his balance on two feet. The same was true of the child who was found in 1694 in the forests of Lithuania, and who lived among bears. He gave no sign of reason, says M. de Condillac, walked on his hands and feet, had no language, and formed sounds having no resemblance whatever to those of a man.[63] The little savage of Hanover, who was taken to the court of England some years ago, had all the trouble in the world to make himself walk on two feet; and in 1719 two other savages, found in the Pyrenees, ran through the mountains in the manner of quadrupeds. As for the objection one could make that this deprives man of the use of his hands, from which we derive so many advantages, besides the example of monkeys, which shows that the hand can very well be used in both ways, it would prove only that man can give his limbs a destination more useful than that of nature, and not that nature destined man to walk otherwise than it teaches him to do.[64]

But there are, it seems to me, far better reasons to state in affirming that man is a biped. First, even if it is shown that he could originally have been formed otherwise than we see him and nonetheless finally become what he is, this would not be enough to conclude that it happened thus; for, after having shown the possibility of these changes, it would still be necessary, before accepting them, at least to demonstrate their probability. Furthermore, if man's arms apparently were able to serve as legs when needed, this is the only observation favorable to that system, against a great number of others which are opposed to it. The principal ones are that the manner in which man's head is attached to his body, instead of directing his sight horizontally—as do all the other animals, and as he himself does when walking erect—would have kept him, walking on all fours, with his eyes directly fastened on the ground, a situation but little favorable to the preservation of the individual; that the tail he lacks, and of which he has no need walking on two feet, is useful to quadrupeds, and none of them is deprived of one; that the breast of a woman, very well placed for a biped who holds her child in her arms, is so badly placed for a quadruped that none has it that way; that the rear quarters being of an excessive height in proportion to the forelegs—so that when walking on all fours we crawl on our knees—the whole would have been an animal ill proportioned and walking uncomfortably; that if he had set his foot down flat as well as the hand, he would have had one less articulation in the posterior leg than do other animals, namely the one that joins the canon bone to the tibia; and that setting down only the tip of the foot, as he doubtless would have been constrained to do, the tarsus—without speaking of the plurality of bones composing it—seems too large to take the place of the canon bone, and its articulations with the metatarsus and the tibia too close together to give the human leg, in this position, the same flexibility as those of quadrupeds. The example of children, as it is taken from an age when natural forces are not as yet developed nor the limbs strengthened, proves nothing whatever; and I might as well say that dogs are not destined to walk because they only crawl several weeks after their birth. Particular facts also have little force against the universal practice of all men, even nations that, having had no communication with others, could not have imitated anything from them. A child abandoned in a forest before he is able to walk, and nourished by some beast, will have followed the example of his nurse in training himself to walk like her; habit could have given him dexterity he did not have from nature; and as armless people succeed, by dint of training, in doing everything with their feet that we do with our hands, he will finally have succeeded in using his hands as feet.

Page 105 (d) Should there be found among my readers a bad enough physical scientist to raise difficulties about the supposition of this natural fertility of the earth, I am going to answer him with the following passage:

"As plants draw much more substance for their nourishment from air and water than they draw from the earth, it happens that when they rot they return more to the earth than they took from it; besides, a forest retains the waters from rain by stopping vapors. Thus, in woods that had been preserved for a long time without being touched, the layer of earth that serves for vegetation would augment considerably; but as animals give back less than they take from the earth, and as men consume enormous quantities of wood and plants for fire and other uses, it follows that the layer of vegetative earth in an inhabited country must always diminish and finally become like the terrain of Arabia Petraea,[65] and like that of so many other provinces of the East—which is in fact the region of most ancient habitation—where only salt and sand are found. For the fixed salt of plants and animals remains, while all the other parts are volatilized." M. de Buffon, HIST. NAT.[66]

To this one can add factual proof from the quantity of trees and plants of all kinds covering almost all the deserted islands discovered in recent centuries, and from what history teaches us about the immense forests that had to be felled all over the earth as it was populated or civilized. On these things I shall further make the following three remarks. First, if there is a kind of vegetation that can compensate for the loss of vegetable matter brought about by animals according to M. de Buffon's reasoning, it is above all woods, the tops and leaves of which collect and appropriate more water and vapors than other plants do. Second, destruction of the soil, that is to say, the loss of the substance suited to vegetation, must accelerate in proportion as the earth is more cultivated and as more industrious inhabitants consume in greater abundance its products of all kinds. My third and most important remark is that the fruits of trees furnish animals with more abundant food than other forms of vegetation can: an experiment I made myself, by comparing the products of two fields equal in size and quality, the one covered with chestnut trees and the other sown with wheat.

Page 106 (e) Among the quadrupeds, the two most universal distinguishing characteristics of voracious species are derived from the shape of the teeth, and the conformation of the intestines. Animals that live only on vegetation all have blunt teeth, like the horse, ox, sheep, hare; but voracious animals have pointed ones, like the cat, dog, wolf, fox. And as for the intestines, the frugivorous ones have some, such as the colon, that are not found in voracious animals. It therefore seems that man, having teeth and intestines like those of frugivorous animals, should naturally be placed in that class; and not only do anatomical observations confirm this opinion, but the great works of antiquity are also very favorable to it. "Dicaearchus,"[67] says Saint Jerome, "relates in his books on Greek antiquities that under the reign of Saturn, when the earth was still fertile by itself, no man ate flesh, but that all lived on fruits and vegetables which grew naturally." (Lib. 2. *Adv. Jovinian.*)[68] That opinion can also be confirmed by the reports of several modern travelers. François Corréal, among others, testifies that most of the inhabitants of the Lucayes whom the Spanish transported to the islands of Cuba, Santo Domingo, and elsewhere, died from having eaten flesh. From this it may be seen that I neglect many favorable points I could exploit. For as prey is almost the unique subject of fighting among carnivorous animals, and as frugivorous ones live among themselves in continual peace, if the human race were of this latter genus it clearly would have had much greater ease subsisting in the state of nature, and much less need and occasion to leave it.

Page 107 (*f*) All knowledge that requires reflection, all knowledge acquired only by the linking of ideas and perfected only successively, seems to be altogether beyond the reach of savage man for want of communication with his fellow men—that is to say, for want of the instrument which is used for that communication and for want of the needs which make it necessary. His knowledge and his industry are limited to jumping, running, fighting, throwing a stone, scaling a tree. But if he knows only these things, in return he knows them much better than we, who do not have the same need of them as he does; and since they depend solely on bodily exercise and are not susceptible of any communication or progress from one individual to another, the first man could have been just as skillful at them as his last descendants.

The reports of travelers are full of examples of the strength and vigor of men in barbarous and savage nations; they praise scarcely less their dexterity and nimbleness: and as eyes alone are needed to observe these things, nothing prevents our giving credence to what eye witnesses certify about them.[69] I draw some examples at random from the first books that come to hand.

"The Hottentots," says Kolben, "understand fishing better than the Europeans of the Cape. They are equally skilled with net, hook, and barb, in coves as well as in rivers. They catch fish by hand no less skillfully. They are incomparably dextrous at swimming. Their manner of swimming has something surprising about it, which is altogether peculiar to them. They swim with their body upright and their hands stretched out of the water, so that they appear to be walking on land. In the greatest agitation of the sea, when the waves form so many mountains, they somehow dance on the crest of the waves, rising and falling like a piece of cork.[70]

"The Hottentots," the same author says further, "have surprising dexterity at hunting, and the nimbleness of their running surpasses the imagination." He is amazed that they do not more often put their agility to bad use, which sometimes happens, however, as can be judged from the example he gives. "A Dutch sailor, disembarking at the Cape," he says, "engaged a Hottentot to follow him to the city with a roll of tobacco weighing about twenty pounds. When they were both at some distance from the crew, the Hottentot asked the sailor if he knew how to run. Run? answered the Dutchman; yes, very well. Let us see, replied the African; and fleeing with the tobacco, he disappeared almost immediately. The sailor, astounded by such marvelous speed, did not think of chasing him, and he never again saw either his tobacco or his porter.

"They have such quick sight and such a sure hand that Europeans cannot come close to them. At a hundred paces they will hit a mark the size of a half-penny with a stone; and what is more astonishing, instead of fixing their eyes on the target, as we do, they make continuous movements and contortions. It seems that their stone is carried by an invisible hand."[71]

Father du Tertre says, concerning the savages of the Antilles, approximately the same things that have just been read concerning the Hottentots of the Cape of Good Hope. He praises above all their accuracy in shooting, with arrows, flying birds and swimming fish, which they then catch by diving. The savages of North America are no less famous for their strength and dexterity, and here is an example that will permit us to judge that of the Indians of South America.

In the year 1746, an Indian from Buenos Aires, having been condemned to the galleys at Cadiz, proposed to the governor that he redeem his freedom by risking his life at a public festival. He promised that by himself he would attack the fiercest bull with no other weapon in hand than a rope; that he would bring it to the ground, seize it with his rope by whatever part they would indicate, saddle it, bridle it, mount it, and so mounted, fight two other bulls of the fiercest kind to be let out of the Torillo; and that he would put them all to death, one after another, at the instant they would command him to do so, and without help from anyone. This was granted him. The Indian kept his word, and succeeded in everything he had promised. On the way in which he did it and on all the detail of the fight, one can consult the first volume, in-12°, of *Observations sur l'histoire naturelle* by M. Gautier, page 262, from which this fact is taken.[72]

Page 109 (*g*) "The length of the life of horses," says M. de Buffon, "as in all other species of animals, is proportionate to the length of time of their growth. Man, who takes fourteen years to grow, can live six or seven times as long, that is to say ninety or one hundred years; the horse, whose growth is completed in four years, can live six or seven times as long, that is to say twenty-five or thirty years. The examples that could be contrary to this rule are so rare that they should not even be considered as an exception from which conclusions can be drawn; and just as heavy horses reach their growth in less time than delicate horses, so they live less time, and are old from the age of fifteen."[73]

Page 109 (*h*) I believe I see another difference between carnivorous and frugivorous animals which is still more general than the one I remarked upon in note (*e*), since this one extends to birds. This difference consists in the number of young, which never exceeds two in each litter for the species that live only on vegetables, and which ordinarily goes beyond this number for voracious animals. It is easy to know nature's design in this regard by the number of teats, which is only two in each female of the first species, like the mare, cow, goat, doe, ewe, etc. and which is always six or eight in the other females, like the bitch, cat, wolf, tigress, etc. The hen, goose, duck, which are all voracious birds, as are the eagle, sparrow-hawk, screech-owl, also lay and hatch a large number of eggs, which never happens to the pigeon, turtle-dove, nor to birds that eat absolutely nothing except grain, which hardly ever lay and hatch more than two eggs at a time. The reason that can be given for this difference is that animals that live only on grasses and plants, remaining almost the entire day at pasture and being forced to spend much time nourishing themselves, could not be adequate to the nursing of several young; whereas voracious ones, having their meal almost in an instant, can more easily and more frequently return to their young and their hunting, and compensate for the dissipation of such a large quantity of milk. There would be many particular observations and reflections to make about all this, but this is not the place for them, and it is sufficient for me to have shown in this part the most general system of nature, a system which furnishes a new reason to withdraw man from the class of carnivorous animals and to place him among the frugivorous species.

Page 115 (i) A famous author calculating the goods and evils of human life, and comparing the two sums, found that the latter greatly surpassed the former, and that all things considered life was a rather poor present to man. I am not surprised by his conclusion; he drew all his reasons from the constitution of civil man. If he had gone back to natural man, it can be concluded that he would have found very different results; he would have perceived that man has hardly any evils other than those he has given himself, and that nature would have been justified. It is not without difficulty that we have succeeded in making ourselves so unhappy. When, on the one hand, one considers the vast labors of men, so many sciences fathomed, so many arts invented, and so many forces employed, chasms filled, mountains razed, rocks broken, rivers made navigable, land cleared, lakes dug out, swamps drained, enormous buildings raised upon the earth, the sea covered with ships and sailors; and when, on the other hand, one searches with a little meditation for the true advantages that have resulted from all this for the happiness of the human species, one cannot fail to be struck by the astounding disproportion prevailing between these things, and to deplore man's blindness, which, to feed his foolish pride and an indefinable vain admiration for himself, makes him run avidly after all the miseries of which he is susceptible, and which beneficent nature had taken care to keep from him.[74]

Men are wicked; sad and continual experience spares the need for proof. However, man is naturally good; I believe I have demonstrated it. What then can have depraved him to this extent, if not the changes that have befallen his constitution, the progress he has made, and the knowledge he has acquired? Let human society be as highly admired as one wants; it is nonetheless true that it necessarily brings men to hate each other in proportion to the conflict of their interests, to render each other apparent services and in fact do every imaginable harm to one another. What is to be thought of intercourse in which the reason of each individual dictates to him maxims directly contrary to those that public reason preaches to the body of society, and in which each man finds his profit in the misfortune of others? There is perhaps no well-to-do man whose death is not secretly hoped for by avid heirs and often his own children; no ship at sea whose wreck would not be good news to some merchant; no firm that a debtor of bad faith would not wish to see burned along with all the papers it contains; no people that does not rejoice about the disasters of its neighbors. Thus do we find our advantage in the detriment of our fellow-men, and someone's loss almost always creates another's prosperity. But what is still more dangerous is that public calamities are awaited and hoped for by a multitude of individuals. Some want illnesses, others death, others war, others famine. I have seen atrocious men weep with sadness at the probability of a fertile year; and the great and deadly fire of London, which cost the life or goods of so many unfortunates, perhaps made the fortune of more than ten thousand people. I know that Montaigne blames the Athenian Demades for having had a worker punished who, by selling coffins at a high price, gained a great deal from the death of citizens. But as the reason Montaigne advances is that everyone would have to be punished, it is evident that it confirms my own.[75] Let us therefore perceive, through our frivolous demonstrations of good will, what goes on at the bottom of our hearts, and let us reflect on what the state of things must be where all men are forced to flatter and destroy one another, and where they are born enemies by duty and swindlers by interest. If I am answered that society is so constituted that each man gains by serving the others, I shall reply that this would be very well, if he did not gain still more by harming them. There is no profit, however legitimate, that is not surpassed by one that can be made illegitimately, and wrong done to one's neighbor is always more lucrative than services. Therefore it is no longer a question of anything except finding ways to be assured of impunity; and it is for this that the powerful use all their strength and the weak all their ruses.

Savage man, when he has eaten, is at peace with all nature, and the friend of all his fellow-men. If it is sometimes a question of disputing his meal, he never comes to blows without first having compared the difficulty of winning with that of finding his subsistence elsewhere; and as pride is not involved in the fight, it is ended by a few blows; the victor eats, the vanquished goes off to seek his fortune, and all is pacified. But for man in society these are altogether different affairs: it is first of all a question of providing for the necessary, and then for the superfluous; next come delights, then immense wealth, and then subjects, and then slaves; he does not have a moment of respite. What is most singular is that the less natural and urgent the needs, the more the passions augment, and, what is worse, the power to satisfy them; so that after long prosperity, after having swallowed up many treasures and desolated many men, my hero will end by ruining everything until he is the sole master of the universe. Such in brief is the moral picture, if not of human life, at least of the secret pretensions of the heart of every civilized man.

Compare, without prejudices, the state of civil man with that of savage man, and seek if you can how many new doors—other than his wickedness, his needs, and his miseries—the former has opened to suffering and death. If you consider the mental anguish that consumes us, the violent passions that exhaust and desolate us, the excessive labors with which the poor are overburdened, the still more dangerous softness to which the rich abandon themselves, and which cause the former to die of their needs and the latter of their excesses; if you think of the monstrous mixtures of foods, their pernicious seasonings, corrupted foodstuffs, falsified drugs, the knavery of those who sell them, the errors of those who administer them, the poison of the containers in which they are prepared; if you pay attention to the epidemic illnesses engendered by the bad air among the multitudes of men gathered together, to the illnesses occasioned by the delicacy of our way of life, by the alternating movements from the interior of our houses into the fresh air, the use of garments put on or taken off with too little precaution, and all the cares that our excessive sensuality has turned into necessary habits, the neglect or privation of which then costs us our life or our health; if you take into account fires and earthquakes which, burning or upsetting whole cities, cause their inhabitants to die by the thousands; in a word, if you unite the dangers that all these causes continually gather over our heads, you will sense how dearly nature makes us pay for the scorn we have shown for its lessons.

I shall not repeat here what I have said elsewhere about war;[76] but I wish that informed men wanted or dared, for once, to give the public the detail of the horrors committed in armies by supply and hospital entrepreneurs. One would see that their not overly secret maneuvers, because of which the most brilliant armies dissolve into less than nothing, cause more soldiers to perish than are cut down by the enemy's sword. It is no less astonishing, further, to calculate the men swallowed up by the sea every year, either by hunger, or scurvy, or pirates, or fire, or shipwreck. It is clear that to established property, and consequently to society, must be attributed the assassinations, poisonings, highway robberies, and even the punishments of these crimes: punishments that are necessary to prevent greater evils, but which, costing the lives of two or more for the murder of one man, nevertheless actually double the loss to the human species. How many shameful ways there are to prevent the birth of men and trick nature; either by those brutal and depraved tastes that insult its most charming work, tastes that neither savages nor animals ever knew and that have arisen in civilized countries only from a corrupt imagination; or by those secret abortions, worthy fruits of debauchery and vicious honor; or by the exposure or murder of a multitude of infants, victims of the misery of their parents or the barbarous shame of their mothers; or, finally, by the mutilation of those unfortunates, for whom a part of their existence and all their posterity are sacrificed to vain songs or, worse yet, to the brutal jealousy of a few men: a mutilation which, in this last case, doubly outrages nature, both by the treatment given those who suffer it and by the use to which they are destined!

But are there not a thousand more frequent and even more dangerous cases in which paternal rights openly offend humanity? How many talents are buried and inclinations forced by the imprudent constraint of fathers! How many men would have distinguished themselves in an appropriate status who die unhappy and dishonored in another status for which they had no taste! How many happy but unequal marriages have been broken or disturbed, and how many chaste wives dishonored, by this order of conditions always in contradiction with that of nature! How many other bizarre unions formed by interest and disavowed by love and reason! How many even honest and virtuous spouses torture one another because of being ill-mated! How many young and unhappy victims of their parents' avarice plunge into vice or spend their sad days in tears, and groan in indissoluble chains which the heart rejects and which gold alone has formed! Happy sometimes are those women whose courage and even virtue tear them from life before barbarous violence forces them into crime or despair. Forgive me, father and mother forever deplorable: I regretfully embitter your suffering; but may it serve as an eternal and terrible example to whomever dares, in the very name of nature, to violate the most sacred of its rights!

If I have spoken only of those ill-formed unions that are the product of our civilization, is it to be thought that those over which love and sympathy have presided are themselves without disadvantages? What would happen if I undertook to show the human species attacked at its very source, and even in the most holy of all bonds, where one no longer dares to listen to nature until after consulting his fortune, and where, with civil disorder confusing virtues and vices, continence becomes a criminal precaution and the refusal to give life to one's fellow-man an act of humanity? But without tearing off the veil that covers so many horrors, let us be content to indicate the evil for which others must furnish the remedy.

Add to all this that quantity of unhealthy trades which shorten lives or destroy the physique, such as labor in mines, various preparations of metals and minerals, especially lead, copper, mercury, cobalt, arsenic, realgar; those other perilous trades which daily cost the life of a number of workers, some of them roofers, others carpenters, others masons, others working in quarries; gather all these things together, I say, and one will be able to see in the establishment and perfection of societies the reasons for the diminution of the species observed by more than one philosopher.[77]

Luxury, impossible to prevent among men greedy for their own commodities and the esteem of others, soon completes the evil that societies began; and on the pretext of keeping the poor alive, which it was not necessary to do, luxury impoverishes everyone else, and depopulates the State sooner or later.

Luxury is a remedy far worse than the evil it claims to cure; or rather it is itself the worst of all evils in any State whatever, whether large or small, and in order to feed the crowds of lackeys and miserable people it has created, it crushes and ruins the farmer and the citizen, like those burning winds in the south which, covering the grass and greenery with devouring insects, take subsistence away from useful animals, and bring famine and death to every place where they make themselves felt.

From society and the luxury it engenders arise the liberal and mechanical arts, commerce, letters, and all those useless things which make industry flourish, enrich and ruin States. The reason for this deterioration is very simple. It is easy to see that, by its nature, agriculture must be the least lucrative of all the arts, because its product being of the most indispensable use to all men, its price must be in proportion to the abilities of the poorest. From the same principle can be drawn this rule: in general the arts are lucrative in inverse ratio to their utility, and the most necessary must finally become the most neglected. From this one sees what must be thought of the true advantages of industry and of the real effect that results from its progress.

Such are the perceptible causes of all the miseries into which opulence finally precipitates the most admired nations. As industry and the arts spread and flower, the scorned cultivator, burdened with taxes necessary for the maintenance of luxury and condemned to spend his life between labor and hunger, abandons his fields to go to the cities in search of the bread he ought to carry there. The more capital cities impress the stupid eyes of the people as admirable, the more it will be necessary to groan at the sight of the abandoned countryside, fallow fields, and main routes flooded with unhappy citizens who have become beggars or thieves, destined to end their misery one day on the rack or on a dung-heap. Thus the State, enriching itself on one hand, weakens and depopulates itself on the other, and thus the most powerful monarchies, after much labor to become opulent and deserted, end by becoming the prey of poor nations which succumb to the deadly temptation to invade them, and which grow rich and weak in their turn, until they are themselves invaded and destroyed by others.

Let someone deign to explain to us for once what

could have produced those hordes of barbarians who, for so many centuries, inundated Europe, Asia, and Africa. Was it to the industry of their arts, the wisdom of their laws, and the excellence of their civil order that they owed that prodigious population? Let our learned men have the goodness to tell us why, far from multiplying to that point, those ferocious and brutal men, without enlightenment, without restraint, without education, did not all murder one another at every moment in disputing their food or game. Let them explain how these miserable men had even the boldness to look in the eye such clever men as we were, with such fine military discipline, such fine codes and such wise laws; and why, finally, after society was perfected in the countries of the north, and so many pains taken there to teach men their mutual duties and the art of living together agreeably and peaceably, nothing more is seen to come from them like those multitudes of men it produced formerly. I am very fearful that someone may finally think of answering me that all these great things, namely the arts, sciences, and laws, have been very wisely invented by men as a salutary plague to prevent the excessive multiplication of the species, for fear that this world, which is destined for us, might finally become too small for its inhabitants.

What! must we destroy societies, annihilate thine and mine, and go back to live in forests with bears? A conclusion in the manner of my adversaries, which I prefer to anticipate rather than leave them the shame of drawing it. Oh you, to whom the heavenly voice has not made itself heard and who recognize no other destination for your species than to end this brief life in peace; you who can leave your fatal acquisitions,

your worried minds, your corrupt hearts, and your unbridled desires in the midst of cities; reclaim, since it
is up to you, your ancient and first innocence; go into
the woods to lose sight and memory of the crimes of
your contemporaries, and have no fear of debasing your
species in renouncing its enlightenment in order to
renounce its vices. As for men like me, whose passions
have forever destroyed their original simplicity, who
can no longer nourish themselves on grass and nuts,
nor do without laws and chiefs; those who were
honored in their first father with supernatural lessons;[78]
those who will see, in the intention of giving human
actions a morality from the start which they would
not have acquired for a long time, the reason for a precept indifferent in itself and inexplicable in any other
system;[79] those, in a word, who are convinced that the
divine voice called the whole human race to the enlightenment and happiness of celestial Intelligences:
all those will endeavor, through the exercise of virtues
they obligate themselves to practice while learning to
know them, to deserve the eternal reward they ought to
expect from them; they will respect the sacred bonds
of the societies of which they are members; they will
love their fellow-men and will serve them with all their
power; they will scrupulously obey the laws, and the
men who are their authors and ministers; they will
honor above all the good and wise princes who will
know how to prevent, cure, or palliate that multitude
of abuses and evils always ready to crush us; they will
animate the zeal of these worthy chiefs, by showing
them without fear and flattery the greatness of their
task and the rigor of their duty. But they will nonetheless scorn a constitution that can be maintained

only with the help of so many respectable people—
who are desired more often than obtained—and from
which, despite all their care, always arise more real
calamities than apparent advantages.[80]

Page 115 (j) Among the men we know, whether
by ourselves, from historians, or from travelers, some
are black, others white, others red; some wear their
hair long, others have only curly wool; some are almost
entirely hairy, others do not even have a beard. There
have been, and there perhaps still are, nations of men
of gigantic size; and apart from the fable of the Pyg-
mies, which may well be only an exaggeration, it is
known that the Laplanders, and above all the Greenlanders, are well below the average size of man. It is
even claimed that there are whole peoples that have
tails like quadrupeds. And without accepting in blind
faith the reports of Herodotus and Ctesias, one can at
least draw from them this very likely opinion: if one
had been able to make good observations in those
ancient times when various peoples followed ways of
life with greater differences between them than peoples do today, one would also have noted, in the shape
and habits of the body, much more striking varieties.
All these facts, for which it is easy to furnish incontestable proofs, can surprise only those who are accustomed to look solely at the objects surrounding
them, and who are ignorant of the powerful effects of
the diversity of climates, air, foods, way of life, habits
in general, and above all the astonishing force of the
same causes when they act continually upon long se-
quences of generations. Today when commerce, voyages, and conquests unite various peoples more, and
their ways of life are constantly brought closer to-

gether by frequent communication, it is perceived that certain national differences have diminished; and, for example, everyone can see that the French of today are no longer those large, pale, and blond-haired bodies described by Latin historians, although time, together with the admixture of the Francs and Normans, themselves pale and blond-haired, ought to have re-established what the frequentation of the Romans could have removed from the influence of the climate in the natural constitution and complexion of the inhabitants. All these observations upon the varieties that a thousand causes can produce and have in fact produced in the human species make me wonder whether various animals similar to men, taken by travelers for beasts without much examination, either because of a few differences they noted in exterior conformation or solely because these animals did not speak, would not in fact be true savage men whose race, dispersed in the woods in ancient times, had not had an opportunity to develop any of its potential faculties, had not acquired any degree of perfection, and was still found in the primitive state of nature. Let me give an example of what I mean.

"In the kingdom of the Congo," says the translator of the *Histoire des voyages*, "are found many of those large animals called orangutan in the East Indies, which are a sort of middle point between the human species and the baboons. Battel relates that in the forests of Mayomba, in the kingdom of Loango, two kinds of monsters are seen, of which the larger are named *pongos* and the others *enjocos*. The former resemble man exactly, but they are much heavier and very tall. With a human face, they have very deep-set eyes.

Their hands, cheeks and ears are hairless, except for eyebrows which are very long. Although the rest of their body is rather hairy, the hair is not very thick, and its color is brown. Finally, the only part that distinguishes them from men is their leg, which has no calf. They walk upright, holding each other by the hair of the neck; their retreat is in the woods; they sleep in trees, and there they make a kind of roof which shelters them from rain. Their foods are fruits or wild nuts. They never eat flesh. The custom of Negroes who cross the forests is to light fires during the night; they note that in the morning, at their departure, the pongos take their place around the fire, and do not withdraw until it is out; for with all their cleverness, they do not have enough sense to keep it going by bringing wood to it.

"They sometimes walk in groups and kill Negroes who cross the forests. They even fall upon elephants that come to graze in the places they inhabit, and annoy them so with punches or sticks that they force them to flee screaming. Pongos are never taken alive because they are so robust that ten men would not suffice to stop them. But the Negroes take many young ones after killing the mother, to whose body the young are strongly attached. When one of these animals dies, the others cover its body with a heap of branches or leaves. Purchass adds that in the conversations he had with Battel he learned from him that a pongo kidnapped a little Negro who spent a whole month in the society of these animals, for they do no harm to men they take by surprise, at least when the latter do not pay attention to them, as the little Negro had observed. Battel did not describe the second species of monster.

"Dapper confirms that the kingdom of the Congo is full of those animals which in the Indies have the name orangutans, that is to say, inhabitants of the woods, and which the Africans call *quojas morros*. This beast, he says, is so similar to man that it came to the mind of some travelers that it might have issued from a woman and a monkey: a chimera which even the Negroes reject. One of these animals was transported from the Congo to Holland, and presented to the Prince of Orange, Frederick-Henry. It was the height of a three-year-old child, and moderately stout but square and well-proportioned, very agile and lively, its legs fleshy and robust, the whole front of its body naked but the back covered with black hair. At first sight its face resembled that of a man, but it had a flat and curved nose; its ears were also those of the human species; its breast, for it was a female, was plump, its navel deep, its shoulders very well joined, its hands divided into fingers and thumbs, its calves and heels fat and fleshy. It often walked upright on its legs, it was able to lift and carry rather heavy loads. When it wanted to drink, it took the cover of the pot in one hand, and held the base with the other, afterward it graciously wiped its lips. It lay down to sleep with its head on a pillow, covering itself so skillfully that one would have taken it for a man in bed. The Negroes tell strange tales about this animal. They assert not only that it does violence to women and girls, but that it dares to attack armed men. In a word, there is great likelihood that it is the satyr of the ancients. Merolla perhaps speaks of none other than these animals when he relates that Negroes sometimes catch savage men and women in their hunts."[81]

These species of anthropomorphic animals are spoken of again in the third volume of the same *Histoire des voyages* under the name of *beggos* and *mandrills*. But to limit ourselves to the preceding reports, in the description of these supposed monsters are found striking conformities with the human species and lesser differences than those which could be assigned between one man and another. In these passages one does not see the reasons the authors have for refusing to give the animals in question the name of savage men; but it is easy to guess that it is due to their stupidity and also because they did not talk: weak reasons for those who know that although the organ of speech is natural to man, speech itself is nonetheless not natural to him, and who know to what point his perfectibility can have raised civil man above his original state. The small number of lines these descriptions contain can enable us to judge how badly these animals were observed, and with what prejudices they were seen. For example, they are qualified as monsters, and yet it is agreed that they reproduce. In one place, Battel says that the pongos kill Negroes who cross the forests; in another, Purchass adds that they do not do them any harm, even when they surprise them, at least when the Negroes make no effort to pay attention to them. The pongos gather around fires lit by Negroes when the latter withdraw, and withdraw in turn when the fire is out: there is the fact. Here now is the commentary of the observer: *for with all their cleverness, they do not have enough sense to keep it going by bringing wood to it.* I would like to guess how Battel, or Purchass his compiler, could have known that the withdrawal of the pongos was an effect of their stupidity rather than their will. In a climate such as Loango, fire is not a very necessary thing for animals; and if the Negroes light it, it is less against the cold than to frighten wild beasts. It is therefore a very simple thing that having enjoyed the blaze for some time, or being well warmed, the pongos are bored with always staying in the same place and go off to find food, which requires more time than if they ate flesh. Besides, it is known that most animals, not excepting man, are naturally lazy, and that they deny themselves all kinds of cares that are not of an absolute necessity. Finally, it seems very strange that the pongos whose skill and strength is praised, the pongos who know how to bury their dead and make themselves roofs out of branches, should not know how to push wood into the fire. I remember having seen a monkey perform the same maneuver that it is denied a pongo can do. It is true that my ideas not then being directed to this problem, I myself committed the error for which I reproach our travelers, and I neglected to examine whether the monkey's intention was in fact to sustain the fire or simply, as I believe, to imitate the action of a man. Whatever the case, it is well demonstrated that the monkey is not a variety of man, not only because he is deprived of the faculty of speech, but especially because it is certain that his species does not have the faculty of perfecting itself, which is the specific characteristic of the human species—experiments which do not appear to have been made on the pongo and the orangutan with enough care to allow drawing the same conclusion for them. There would, however, be a means by which, if the orangutan or others were of the human species, the crudest observers could even assure themselves of it by demonstration. But besides the fact that a single generation would not suffice for this experiment, it must pass as impracticable, because it would be necessary that what is only a supposition were shown to be true before the test that ought to verify the fact could be tried innocently.[82]

Precipitous judgments, which are not the fruit of enlightened reason, are liable to be excessive. Without ceremony our travelers take for beasts, under the names *pongos, mandrills, orangutans*, the same beings that the ancients, under the names *satyrs, fauns, sylvans*, took for divinities. Perhaps, after more precise research, it will be found that they are neither animals nor gods, but men.[83] In the meantime, it seems to me that there is as much reason to defer on this subject to Merolla, an educated monk, an eyewitness, and one who, with all his naïveté, was nonetheless a man of wit, as to the merchant Battel, Dapper, Purchass, and the other compilers.

What judgment would such observers have made about the child found in 1694, of whom I spoke before, who gave no sign of reason, walked on his hands and feet, had no language, and formed sounds having no resemblance whatever to those of a man? It took a long time, continues the same philosopher who provided me with this fact,[84] before he could utter a few words, and then he did it in a barbarous way. As soon as he could speak, he was questioned about his first state, but he did not remember it any more than we remember what happened to us in the cradle. If unhappily for him, this child had fallen into the hands of our travelers, it cannot be doubted that after noting his silence and stupidity, they would have decided to send him back to the woods or lock him up in a zoo; after which they would have spoken learnedly of him in splendid reports as a very curious beast which looked rather like man.

For the three or four hundred years since the inhabitants of Europe have inundated the other parts of the world, and continually published new collections of voyages and reports, I am convinced that we know no other men except the Europeans; furthermore, it appears, from the ridiculous prejudices which have not died out even among men of letters, that under the pompous name of the study of man everyone does hardly anything except study the men of his country. In vain do individuals come and go; it seems that philosophy does not travel. In addition, the philosophy of each people is but little suited for another. The cause of this is manifest, at least for distant countries; there are scarcely more than four sorts of men who make voyages of long duration: sailors, merchants, soldiers, and missionaries. Now it can hardly be expected that the first three classes should provide good observers; and as for those in the fourth, occupied by the sublime vocation that calls them, even if they were not subject to the same prejudices of status as are all the others, it must be believed that they would not voluntarily give themselves over to researches that appear to be pure curiosity, and which would distract them from the more important works to which they are destined. Besides, to preach the Gospel usefully, zeal alone is necessary and God gives the rest; but to study men, talents are necessary that God is not obligated to give anyone, and that are not always the lot of saints. One does not open a book of voyages without finding descriptions of characters and customs. But one is completely amazed to see that these people who have described so many things have said only what everyone already knew, that they have known how to perceive, at the other end of the world, only what it was up to them to notice without leaving their street; and that those true features that distinguish nations and strike eyes made to see have almost always escaped theirs. Hence this fine adage of ethics, so often repeated by the philosophical rabble: That men are everywhere the same; that as they have the same passions and the same vices everywhere, it is rather useless to seek to characterize different peoples—which is about as well reasoned as if one were to say it is impossible to distinguish Peter from James, because they both have a nose, a mouth, and eyes.

Shall we never see reborn those happy times when the people did not dabble in philosophy, but when a Plato, a Thales, a Pythagoras, seized with an ardent desire to know, undertook the greatest voyages solely to inform themselves, and went far away to shake off the yoke of national prejudices, to learn to know men by their likenesses and their differences, and to acquire that universal knowledge which is not that of one century or one country exclusively, but which, being of all times and all places, is so to speak the common science of the wise?

One admires the lavishness of some curious people who have, at great expense, made or arranged voyages to the Orient with learned men and painters, to draw pictures of ruins there and to decipher or copy inscriptions. But I have difficulty conceiving how, in a century taking pride in splendid knowledge, there are not to be found two closely united men—rich, one in money and the other in genius, both loving glory and aspiring to immortality—one of whom would sacrifice twenty thousand crowns of his wealth and the other ten years of his life to a celebrated voyage around the world, in order to study, not always stones and plants, but for once men and morals, and who, after so many centuries used to measure and examine the house, should finally make up their minds to want to know its inhabitants.

The academicians who have traveled through the northern parts of Europe and the southern parts of America intended to visit them as geometers rather than as philosophers. However, being both at the same time, the regions that have been seen and described by La Condamine and Maupertuis cannot be considered as entirely unknown. The jeweler Chardin, who traveled like Plato, left nothing to be said about Persia. China appears to have been well observed by the Jesuits. Kempfer gives a passable idea of the little he saw in Japan. With the exception of these reports, we know nothing of the peoples of the East Indies, who have been frequented solely by Europeans more desirous to fill their purses than their heads. All of Africa and its numerous inhabitants, as distinctive in character as in color, are still to be examined; the whole earth is covered by nations of which we know only the names—yet we dabble in judging the human race! Let us suppose a Montesquieu, Buffon, Diderot, Duclos, d'Alembert, Condillac, or men of that stamp traveling in order to inform their compatriots, observing and describing, as they know how, Turkey, Egypt, Barbary, the empire of Morocco, Guinea, the land of the Bantus, the interior of Africa and its eastern coasts, the Malabars, Mogul, the banks of the Ganges, the kingdoms of Siam, Pegu, and Ava, China, Tartary, and especially Japan; then, in the other hemisphere, Mexico, Peru, Chile, the straits of Magellan, not forgetting the Patagonias true or false, Tucuman, Paraguay if possible, Brazil; finally the Caribbean islands, Florida, and all the savage countries: the most important voyage of all and the one that must be undertaken with the greatest care. Let us suppose that these new Hercules, back from these memorable expeditions, then at leisure wrote the natural, moral, and political history of what they would have seen; we ourselves would see a new world come from their pens, and we would thus learn to know our own. I say that when such observers will affirm of a given animal that it is a man and of another that it is a beast, they will have to be believed; but it would be too credulous to defer to crude travelers about whom one would sometimes be tempted to ask the very question that they meddle in resolving concerning other animals.[85]

Page 116 (k) That seems totally evident to me, and I am unable to conceive whence our philosophers can derive all the passions they impute to natural man. With the sole exception of the physically necessary, which nature itself demands, all our other needs are such only by habit, having previously not been needs, or by our desires; and one does not desire that which he is not capable of knowing. From which it follows that savage man, desiring only the things he knows and knowing only those things the possession of which is in his power or easily acquired, nothing should be so tranquil as his soul and nothing so limited as his mind.

Page 121 (l) I find in Locke's On Civil Government

an objection which seems to me too specious for me to be allowed to conceal it.[86] "The end of conjunction between male and female," says this philosopher, "being not barely procreation, but the continuation of the species, this conjunction ought to last, even after procreation, so long as is necessary to the nourishment and support of the young ones, till they are able to shift and provide for themselves. This rule, which the infinite wise Maker hath set to the works of his hands, we find the inferior creatures steadily and exactly obey. In those animals which feed on grass, the conjunction between male and female lasts no longer than the very act of copulation, because the teat of the dam being sufficient to nourish the young till it be able to feed on grass, the male only begets, but concerns not himself for the female or young to whose subsistence he can contribute nothing. But in beasts of prey the conjunction lasts longer, because the dam not being able well to subsist herself and nourish her numerous offspring by her own prey alone, a more laborious as well as more dangerous way of living than by feeding on grass; the assistance of the male is altogether necessary to the maintenance of their common family, if one may use that term, which cannot subsist till they are able to prey for themselves, but by the joint care of male and female. The same is to be observed in all birds (except some domestic ones where plenty of food excuses the cock from feeding and taking care of the young brood), whose young needing food in the nest, the cock and the hen bring it to them, till the young are able to use their wing and provide for themselves.

"And herein, I think, lies the chief, if not the only, reason why the male and female in mankind are tied to a longer conjunction than other creatures, *viz.*, because the female is capable of conceiving, and is commonly with child again and brings forth, too, a new birth, long before the former is out of a dependency for support on his parent's help, and able to shift for himself; whereby the father, who is bound to take care for those he hath begot, and to undertake that care for a long time, is under an obligation to continue in conjugal society with the same woman by whom he has had them, and to remain in that society much longer than other creatures, whose young being able to subsist of themselves before the time of procreation returns again, the conjugal bond dissolves of itself, and they are at complete liberty, till Hymen at his usual anniversary season summons them again to choose new mates. Wherein one cannot but admire the wisdom of the Creator who, having given to man an ability to lay up for the future as well as to supply the present necessity, hath wanted and made it necessary that society of man should be more lasting than of male and female amongst other creatures, that so their industry might be encouraged, and their interest better united, to make provision and lay up goods for their common issue, which uncertain mixture, or easy and frequent solutions of conjugal society would mightily disturb."

The same love of truth which made me sincerely present this objection prompts me to accompany it with a few remarks, if not to resolve it, at least to clarify it.

1. I shall observe first that moral proofs do not have great force in matters of physics, and that they serve rather to give a reason for existing facts than to prove the real existence of those facts. Now such is the kind

of proof Mr. Locke uses in the passage I have just quoted; for although it may be advantageous to the human species for the union between man and woman to be permanent, it does not follow that it was thus established by nature; otherwise it would be necessary to say that nature also instituted civil society, the arts, commerce, and all that is claimed to be useful to men.

2. I do not know where Mr. Locke found out that among animals of prey the society of male and female lasts longer than among those that live on grass, and that the former helps the latter to feed the young: for it is not observed that the dog, cat, bear, or wolf recognize their female better than the horse, ram, bull, stag, or all the other quadrupeds recognize theirs. It seems on the contrary that if the help of the male were necessary to the female to preserve her young, it would be above all in the species that live only on grass, because the mother needs a very long time to graze, and during that entire period she is forced to neglect her brood; whereas the prey of a female bear or wolf is devoured in an instant, and she has more time, without suffering from hunger, to nurse her young. This reasoning is confirmed by an observation upon the relative number of teats and young which distinguishes the carnivorous species from the frugivorous, and about which I spoke in note (h). If this observation is correct and general, as woman has only two teats and rarely produces more than one child at a time, there is one more strong reason to doubt that the human species is naturally carnivorous. So it seems that in order to draw Locke's conclusion, his reasoning would have to be altogether reversed. The same distinction applied to birds is no more solid. For

who can be persuaded that the union of male and female is more durable among vultures and ravens than
among turtle-doves? We have two species of domestic
birds, the duck and the pigeon, which provide us with
examples directly contrary to the system of this author.
The pigeon, which lives only on grain, remains united
with its female, and they nourish their young in common. The duck, whose voracity is known, recognizes
neither its female nor its young, and does nothing to
help with their subsistence; and among hens, a species
hardly less carnivorous, it is not observed that the
rooster troubles himself in the least for the brood. And
if in other species the male shares with the female the
care of nourishing the young, it is because birds, which
cannot fly at first and which the mother cannot nurse,
are less able to do without the assistance of the father
than are quadrupeds, for which the mother's teat suffices, at least for some time.

3. There is much uncertainty about the principal fact
that serves as a basis for all of Mr. Locke's reasoning:
for in order to know whether, as he claims, in the pure
state of nature the woman is ordinarily pregnant again
and has another child long before the preceding one
can himself provide for his needs, it would be necessary
to make experiments that Mr. Locke surely did not
make and that no one is able to make. The continual
cohabitation of husband and wife provides such an
immediate opportunity to be exposed to a new pregnancy that it is very hard to believe that chance encounter or the impulsion of temperament alone produced such frequent effects in the pure state of nature
as in the state of conjugal society—a slowness which
would perhaps tend to make the children more robust,

and which in addition might be compensated by a prolonged ability to conceive among women, who would have abused it less in their youth. With regard to children, there are many reasons to believe that their strength and their organs develop later among us than they did in the primitive state of which I speak. The original weakness they derive from the constitution of their parents, the cares taken to wrap and restrain all their limbs, the softness in which they are raised, perhaps the use of milk other than their mother's, everything opposes and retards in them the first progress of nature. The concentration they are obliged to give to a thousand things on which their attention is continually fixed, while no exercise is given to their bodily strength, may also bring about considerable diversion in their growth; so that if instead of first overburdening and tiring their minds in a thousand ways, their bodies were left to be exercised by the continual movements that nature seems to demand of them, it is to be presumed that they would much sooner be capable of walking, acting, and providing for their needs themselves.[87]

4. Finally, Mr. Locke proves at most that there could well be in a man a motive for remaining attached to a woman when she has a child; but he does not prove at all that he must have been attached to her before the delivery and during the nine months of pregnancy. If a given woman is indifferent to the man during these nine months, if she even becomes unknown to him, why will he assist her after delivery? Why will he help her to raise a child he does not even know belongs to him, and whose birth he neither planned nor foresaw? Mr. Locke evidently supposes

what is in question; for it is not a matter of knowing why the man will remain attached to the woman after delivery, but why he will become attached to her after conception. His appetite satisfied, the man no longer needs a given woman, nor the woman a given man. The man has not the least concern nor perhaps the least idea of the consequences of his action. One goes off in one direction, the other in another, and there is no likelihood that at the end of nine months they have any memory of having known each other: for this kind of memory, by which one individual gives preference to another for the act of procreation, requires, as I prove in the text, more progress or corruption in human understanding than can be supposed in man in the state of animality in question here. Another woman can therefore satisfy the new desires of the man as conveniently as the one he has already known, and another man satisfy in the same way the woman, supposing that she is impelled by the same appetite during pregnancy, which can reasonably be doubted. And if in the state of nature the woman no longer feels the passion of love after the conception of the child, the obstacle to her society with the man thereby becomes much greater still, since then she no longer needs either the man who impregnated her or any other. Therefore there is not, for the man, any reason to seek the same woman, nor for the woman, any reason to seek the same man. Locke's reasoning therefore falls apart, and all the dialectic of this philosopher has not saved him from the error committed by Hobbes and others. They had to explain a fact of the state of nature, that is to say, of a state where men lived isolated and where a given man had no motive for living near another given man, nor perhaps to live near one another, which is much worse; and they did not think of carrying themselves back beyond the centuries of society, that is to say, of those times when men have always had a reason to live near one another, and when a given man often has a reason for living beside a given man or a given woman.[88]

Page 121 (m) I shall refrain from launching into the philosophic reflections to be made about the advantages and inconveniences of this institution of languages: it is not for me to be permitted to attack vulgar errors, and educated people respect their prejudices too much to bear my supposed paradoxes with patience. Let us therefore let men speak who have not been accused of a crime for sometimes daring to take the side of reason against the opinion of the multitude. *Nec quidquam felicitati humani generis decederet, si pulsa tot linguarum peste et confusione, unam artem callerent mortales, et signis, motibus, gestibusque, licitum foret quidvis explicare. Nunc vero ita comparatum est, ut animalium quae vulgo bruta creduntur melior longe quam nostra hac in parte videatur conditio, utpote quae promptius, et forsan felicius, sensus et cogitationes suas sine interprete significent, quam ulli queant mortales, praesertim si peregrino utantur sermone.* (Is. Vossius, *de Poëmat. Cant. et Viribus Rythmi*, p. 66.)[89]

Page 126 (n) Plato, showing how ideas of discrete quantity and its relationships are necessary in the least of arts, with reason makes fun of the authors of his time who claimed that Palamedes had invented numbers at the siege of Troy; as if, says this philosopher, Agamemnon could have been ignorant until then of how many legs he had.[90] In fact, one senses the impossibility for society and the arts to have reached the point where they already were at the time of the siege of Troy unless men had the use of numbers and arithmetic. But the need to know numbers, before acquiring other knowledge, does not make their invention easier to imagine. Once the names of the numbers are known, it is easy to explain their meaning and evoke the ideas these names represent; but in order to invent them it was necessary, before conceiving of these same ideas, to be so to speak familiar with philosophic meditations, to be trained in considering beings by their sole essence and independently of all other perception: a very difficult, very metaphysical, very unnatural abstraction, and one without which, nonetheless, these ideas could never have been carried from one species or genus to another, nor could numbers have become universal. A savage could consider separately his right leg and his left leg, or look at them together under the indivisible idea of a pair, without ever thinking that he had two of them; for the representative idea which depicts an object to us is one thing, and the numerical idea which determines it is another. He was even less able to count to five; and although, placing his hands on one another, he could have noticed that the fingers corresponded exactly, he was very far from thinking of their numerical equality. He did not know the sum of his fingers any more than that of his hairs; and if, after having made him understand what numbers are, someone said to him that he had as many toes as fingers, he would perhaps have been very surprised, in comparing them, to find it was true.

Page 130 (o) Vanity and love of oneself, two passions very different in their nature and their effects, must not be confused. Love of oneself is a natural sentiment which inclines every animal to watch over its own preservation, and which, directed in man by reason and modified by pity, produces humanity and virtue. Vanity is only a relative sentiment, artificial and born in society, which inclines each individual to have a greater esteem for himself than for anyone else, inspires in men all the harm they do to one another, and is the true source of honor.

This being well understood, I say that in our primitive state, in the true state of nature, vanity does not exist; for each particular man regarding himself as the sole spectator to observe him, as the sole being in the universe to take an interest in him, and as the sole judge of his own merit, it is not possible that a sentiment having its source in comparisons he is not capable of making could spring up in his soul. For the same reason this man could have neither hate nor desire for revenge, passions that can arise only from the opinion that some offense has been received; and as it is scorn or intention to hurt and not the harm that constitutes the offense, men who know neither how to evaluate themselves nor compare themselves can do each other a great deal of mutual violence when they derive some advantage from it, without ever offending one another. In a word, every man, seeing his fellow-men hardly otherwise than he would see animals of another species, can carry off the prey of the weaker or relinquish his own to the stronger, without considering these plunderings as anything but natural events, without the slightest emotion of insolence or spite, and with no other passion than the sadness or joy of a good or bad outcome.

Page 151 (*p*) It is an extremely remarkable thing, for all the years that Europeans have been tormenting themselves to bring the savages of various countries in the world to their way of life, that they have not yet been able to win over a single one, not even with the aid of Christianity; for our missionaries sometimes make Christians of them, but never civilized men. Nothing can overcome the invincible repugnance they have against adopting our morals and living in our way. If these poor savages are as unhappy as it is claimed they are, by what inconceivable depravity of judgment do they constantly refuse to civilize themselves by imitating us or to learn to live happily among us; whereas one reads in a thousand places that Frenchmen and other Europeans have voluntarily taken refuge among these nations, spent their entire lives there, no longer able to leave such a strange way of life; and whereas one sees even sensible missionaries touchingly regret the calm and innocent days they have spent among such greatly scorned peoples? If one answers that they do not have enough intellect to judge soundly about their state and ours, I shall reply that the estimation of happiness is less the concern of reason than of sentiment. Besides, this reply can be turned against us with even more force; for there is a greater distance between our ideas and the mental disposition necessary in order to conceive of the taste that savages find for their way of life than between the ideas of savages and those that can allow them to conceive of our way of life. In fact, after several observations it is easy for them to see that all our labors are directed toward only two objects: namely, the commodities of life for oneself, and consideration among others. But how are we to imagine the kind of pleasure a savage takes in spending his life alone in the middle of the woods, or fishing, or blowing into a bad flute, without ever knowing how to get a single tone from it and without troubling himself to learn?

Several times savages have been brought to Paris, London, and other cities; men have hurried to show off our luxury, our wealth, and all our most useful and curious arts; all this has never aroused in them anything except stupid admiration, without the slightest emotion of covetousness. I recall among others the story of a chief of some North Americans who was brought to the court of England some thirty years ago. A thousand things were put before his eyes to try to give him some present that could please him, but nothing could be found about which he seemed to care. Our weapons seemed heavy and inconvenient to him; our shoes hurt his feet, our clothes confined him, he refused everything; finally someone observed that having taken a woolen blanket, he seemed to take pleasure in wrapping it around his shoulders. You will at least agree, someone promptly said to him, about the usefulness of this article? Yes, he replied, it seems to me almost as good as an animal skin. And he would not even have said that if he had worn them both in the rain.

Perhaps, someone will say to me, it is habit which, by attaching everyone to his way of life, prevents savages from sensing what is good in ours. And on that basis it must at least appear very extraordinary that habit has more strength in maintaining the savages' taste for their misery than in maintaining Europeans in the enjoyment of their felicity. But to reply to this last objection with an answer to which there is not a word of rejoinder—without citing all the young savages whom men have tried in vain to civilize, without speaking of the Greenlanders and inhabitants of Iceland, whom men tried to raise and feed in Denmark and all of whom sadness and despair caused to perish, either from languor or in the sea when they tried to swim back to their homeland—I shall be content to cite a single, well-authenticated example, which I offer for the examination of admirers of European civilization.

"All the efforts of the Dutch missionaries at the Cape of Good Hope have never been able to convert a single Hottentot. Van der Stel, governor of the Cape, having taken one from infancy, had him raised in the principles of the Christian religion and in the practice of European customs. He was richly dressed, he was taught several languages, and his progress corresponded very well to the cares taken for his education. The governor, placing great hopes in his intelligence, sent him to the Indies with a general commissioner who employed him usefully in the affairs of the company. He returned to the Cape after the death of the commissioner. A few days after his return, during a visit he paid to some of his Hottentot relatives, he made the decision to divest himself of his European finery in order to clothe himself in a sheepskin. He returned to the fort in this new garb, carrying a package which contained his old clothes; and presenting them to the governor, he made this speech:* *Be so kind, sir, as to understand that I renounce this paraphernalia forever; I renounce also for my entire life the Christian religion; my resolution is to live and die in the religion, ways, and customs of*

---

* See the frontispiece.[91]

my ancestors. The sole favor I ask of you is to let me keep the necklace and cutlass I am wearing; I shall keep them for love of you. Immediately, without awaiting Van der Stel's reply, he escaped by running away, and he was never seen again at the Cape." *Histoire des voyages,* volume 5, page 175.[92]

Page 157 (q) One could object that, in such a disorder, men, instead of stubbornly murdering one another, would have dispersed if there had been no limits to their dispersion. But first, these limits would at least have been those of the world; and if one thinks of the excessive population which results from the state of nature, he will judge that it would not have been long before the earth, in that state, was covered with men, thus forced to remain together. Besides, they would have dispersed if the evil had been rapid, and had it been a change occurring overnight. But they were born under the yoke; they were in the habit of bearing it when they felt its weight, and they were content to wait for the opportunity to shake it off. Finally, as they were already accustomed to a thousand commodities which forced them to remain together, dispersion was no longer so easy as in the first ages, when no one having need of anyone but himself, everyone made his decision without waiting for the consent of another.

Page 160 (r) Marshal de Villars related that, in one of his campaigns, the excessive knavery of a food agent having made the army suffer and complain, he berated him severely and threatened to have him hanged. This threat does not bother me, the knave boldly answered him, and I am very happy to tell you that a man who has a hundred thousand crowns at his disposal does not get hanged. I do not know how it happened, the

Marshal added naïvely, but in fact he was not hanged, although he had deserved it a hundred times.

Page 174 (s) Distributive justice would still be opposed to this rigorous equality of the state of nature, even if it were practicable in civil society; and as all the members of the state owe it services proportionate to their talents and strengths, the citizens in their turn ought to be distinguished and favored in proportion to their services. It is in this sense that a passage of Isocrates must be understood, in which he praises the first Athenians for having well known how to distinguish which was the most advantageous of the two sorts of equality, one of which consists in dividing the same advantages among all citizens indifferently, and the other in distributing them according to each man's merit. These skillful politicians, adds the orator, banishing that unjust equality which establishes no difference between evil and good men, adhered inviolably to that which rewards and punishes everyone according to his merit.[93] But first, no society has ever existed, no matter what degree of corruption societies might have reached, in which no difference between evil and good men was established; and in matters of morals—where the law cannot establish an exact enough measurement to serve as a rule for the magistrate—the law very wisely, in order not to leave the fate or rank of citizens at his discretion, forbids him the judgment of persons, leaving him only that of actions. Only morals as pure as those of the ancient Romans can bear censors; such tribunals would soon have overthrown everything among us. It is up to public esteem to establish the difference between evil and good men. The magistrate is judge only of rigorous right; but the people are the true judges of morals: an upright and even enlightened judge on this point, sometimes deceived but never corrupted. The ranks of citizens therefore ought to be regulated not upon their personal merit, which would be leaving to the magistrates the means of making an almost arbitrary application of the law, but upon the real services that they render to the State, which are susceptible of a more exact estimation.[94]

Editor's Notes to the Second Discourse

1. "Not in corrupt things, but in those which are well ordered in accordance with nature, should one consider that which is natural." *Politics* 1254ᵃ36-38 (Book I, chap. v). The context of this quotation (Aristotle's discussion of natural slavery) should be compared to the *Social Contract*, I, ii-iv.

2. The dedication to the Republic of Geneva was written in 1754, and is dated from Chambéry, where Rousseau stopped on his way to Geneva. His return to his native city was an event of particular importance for Rousseau; the prize-winning essayist was well received there, and on August 1, 1754, he returned to the Protestant faith and regained his Genevan citizenship. Since Rousseau was not formally a citizen of Geneva when the dedication was written, it was not strictly proper for him to speak as he does here. The style of the dedicatory epistle is marked by an often extravagant rhetoric, but beneath the glowing praise of Geneva Rousseau clearly delineates the requirements for the best regime a philosopher could wish for. A complete analysis of this dedication would indicate the extent to which these requirements were not fulfilled by Geneva in the eighteenth century; indeed, a former First Syndic of Geneva wrote Rousseau: "You have followed the movements of your heart in the Dedicatory Epistle, and I fear it will be found that you flatter us too much; you represent us as we ought to be, and not as we are." *Correspondance Générale*, II, 193.

3. The "fatal misunderstandings" to which Rousseau refers were not merely a hypothetical possibility; the history of Geneva had been marked by ill-feeling between the citizen body (who formed the *Conseil Général*, the

highest legally constituted legislative body) and the leading magistrates (the *Petit Conseil*, composed of twenty-five members with life tenure, and the *Conseil des Deuxcents*, elected by the *Petit Conseil*). In 1707 a conspiracy was quelled by the execution of its leader, Pierre Fatio; in 1737-38 a more serious conflict was settled only by the intervention and mediation of Zurich, Bern, and France. The reconciliation was far from "sincere and perpetual": civil strife recurred in 1766-68 and in 1780-82, foreign powers playing an important role in the settlement on each occasion. For Rousseau's own analysis of the constitution of Geneva as it stood after the act of Mediation of 1738, see his *Lettres Écrites de la Montagne*, especially vii-ix.

4. An indication of the irony of this passage may be in order. The Code of Political Edicts, which formed the constitutional basis of the Genevan government, was to have been published by the *Petit Conseil* according to the Act of Mediation of 1738; at the time of Rousseau's writing the Edicts had not been published (nor, in fact, had they been published when the Mediating powers were again called in to arbitrate in 1766). See Vaughan, II, 190.

5. Having addressed his male fellow-citizens of Geneva, Rousseau now turns to the magistrates of the city. Note that while the citizens are addressed as "magnificent, most honored, and *sovereign* lords," the magistrates are only "magnificent and most honored lords"; they are not sovereign. Compare *Social Contract*, III, i, and *Lettres Écrites de la Montagne*, vii.

6. This flattering picture of Rousseau's father is not the least of the exaggerated elements in this Dedication. Isaac Rousseau was a proud, restless, headstrong individual who left Geneva a year after his marriage in order to make watches in Constantinople (where there was a "colony" of Swiss artisans). At his wife's request, the

elder Rousseau returned to Geneva in 1711; Jean-Jacques was born on June 28, 1712. Isaac Rousseau's fun-loving and passionate nature was revealed in quarrels—caused by his penchant for hunting on the lands of Geneva's more solid citizens—which came to the attention of the Consistory. The most important of these arguments, with one Pierre Gautier, led to a sword fight on the streets of Geneva, as a result of which the elder Rousseau fled the city to avoid prosecution. At this time (1724-25), the young Jean-Jacques went to live with the Pastor of Boissy, just outside Geneva; thereafter he was a none-too-diligent apprentice to several tradesmen of Geneva. Although Isaac Rousseau did introduce his son to Plutarch and the classics as well as to novels (see Confessions, Book I [Pléiade, I, 9]), it can be wondered how many "wise lessons" Jean-Jacques received from a father who, having fled Geneva to avoid prosecution, virtually abandoned his twelve-year-old son and had little contact with him thereafter. See F. C. Green, Jean-Jacques Rousseau (Cambridge: University Press, 1955), pp. 1-12, 36.

7. "The aberrations of foolish youth" followed upon Rousseau's disgust for the life of an apprentice engraver. One Sunday (March 14, 1728), returning to Geneva after a walk in the countryside, he found the gates of the city closed. To avoid the kind of beating previously received from his master for such misdeeds, Rousseau resolved to seek his fortune elsewhere. Thus began many years of wandering through Europe, during which Rousseau's experiences were as bizarre as they were varied. Having been directed to Mme. de Warens, a Catholic proselytizer in Annecy, Rousseau was ultimately converted to Catholicism in Turin. Thereafter, Rousseau flitted from one occupation to another: lackey, music-teacher knowing nothing of music, secretary to a somewhat fraudulent Greek Archimandrite seeking alms for the restoration of the Holy Sepulcher, lover of Mme. de Warens (twelve years

his senior), clerk in a survey office, tutor, inventor of a revolutionary system of numerical musical notation, secretary to the French ambassador in Venice, composer, secretary to a wealthy tax-collector, etc. In the course of these extraordinary wanderings, Rousseau managed to educate himself, and after he settled in Paris in 1744, he eked out an existence at the margin of French high society until he gained fame with the prize-winning *First Discourse*. During this period, Rousseau began to live with a simple linen-worker, Thérèse Levasseur, who bore him five children (all of whom, by Rousseau's admission, were abandoned in a foundling home at their birth). Rousseau had good reason to speak of the "aberrations of foolish youth." See *Confessions*, Books i-vii, and Green, *Rousseau*, chaps. i-iii.

8. Compare notes 3 and 4 above.

9. Here Rousseau turns from the civil magistrates of Geneva to its Protestant ministers. One should remember that in Calvinist Geneva, religion was of particular importance; "all religious questions, which were, of course, governmental questions, were examined by the Consistory composed of the pastors and twelve laymen." Daniel Mornet, *Rousseau: l'homme et l'œuvre* (Paris: Hatier-Boivin, 1950), p. 10. On the political role of religion, compare *Social Contract*, IV, viii.

10. Rousseau now turns to the female citizens of Geneva (the word used here is "citoyennes"). Note that, strictly speaking, the "citizens" were but one of the five classes in Geneva, and that the political rights of citizenship (holding the highest magistracies and voting in the *Conseil Général*) were open only to males. For Rousseau's views on women, see *Émile*, Book v.

11. The inscription was "Know Thyself" (*gnôthi seauton*).

12. The reference is to Plato's *Republic* X.611. Note that for Rousseau the comparison of the human soul with

the sea-god Glaucus illuminates the problem of discovering man's "primitive state," whereas for Plato the question is the proof of the immortality of the soul.

13. Jean Jacques Burlamaqui, *Principes du Droit Naturel*, I, i, § 2 (Geneva: Barillot & Fils, 1747), p. 2.

14. "The law of nature is that which she has taught all animals; a law not peculiar to the human race, but shared by all living creatures, whether denizens of the air, the dry land, or the sea. Hence comes the union of male and female, which we call marriage; hence the procreation and rearing of children, for this is a law by the knowledge of which we see even the lower animals are distinguished." J. B. Moyle, trans., *Institutes of Justinian* I, ii, 1 (2nd ed.; Oxford: Clarendon Press, 1889), p. 4. Compare the almost identical formulation of Ulpian quoted by Robert Dérathé, *Jean-Jacques Rousseau et la Science Politique de son Temps* (Paris: Presses Universitaires de France, 1950), p. 388.

15. Rousseau here seems to refer both to modern jurists, like Grotius, Pufendorf, and Barbeyrac, and to Hobbes and Locke. But it is at least possible that Rousseau is thinking most particularly of the former; later in the *Second Discourse* (p. 129) Hobbes is explicitly distinguished from "the moderns." For the views of the "modern jurists," see Hugo Grotius, *Le Droit de la Guerre et de la Paix*, I, i, § 11 (Jean Barbeyrac, trans. [Amsterdam: Pierre de Coup, 1724], pp. 52-53), and Samuel Pufendorf's critique of the notion of natural law in the works of Spinoza and Hobbes in *Le Droit de la Nature et des Gens*, II, ii, esp. § 3 and 9 (Jean Barbeyrac, trans. [Amsterdam: Gerard Kuyper, 1706], pp. 140-44, 150-52). Compare Pufendorf's definition of natural law (*ibid.*, II, iii) with Hobbes's distinction between "rights of nature" and "laws of nature" (*Leviathan*, I, xiii-xiv). Compare also Burlamaqui, *Principes du Droit Naturel*, II, i, § 2 (ed. 1747, p. 142).

234 / SECOND DISCOURSE

16. Compare Pufendorf, who considered "sociability" to be "the fundamental law of natural right." *Le Droit de la Nature et des Gens*, II, iii, § 15 (ed. 1706, I, 178).

17. "Learn whom God has ordered you to be, and in what part of human affairs you have been placed." Persius, *Satires* iii. 71-72. Compare Pufendorf's use of this passage and the Delphic inscription "Know Thyself" in *Le Droit de la Nature et des Gens*, II, iv, § 5 (ed. 1706, I, 210).

18. Elsewhere Rousseau insists on the necessity of reading his books at least twice, which implies that these notes are absolutely essential if one is to understand the *Second Discourse* fully. *Rousseau Juge de Jean-Jacques*, Dialogue iii (Pléiade, I, 932-33). Note also that this passage of the *Dialogues*, by suggesting that Rousseau's works develop his principles in an order which "was retrograde to that of their publication," indicates the *Discourses* are the most complex formulation of Rousseau's thought.

19. Compare the question proposed by the Academy of Dijon with the formulation adopted by Rousseau: reference to the authorization of inequality by natural law is replaced by the "foundations" of inequality.

20. Rousseau's phrase is "des qualités de l'esprit ou de l'âme." At the risk of narrowing the meaning somewhat, the word *esprit* will always be translated "mind" even though it can mean "spirit" or "soul"; *âme* will be rendered by "soul." Compare this list of the natural inequalities among men with the qualities which first give rise to esteem in savage society (p. 149) and with the qualities which determine the "rank and fate of each man" once man has been perfected and civilized (p. 155).

21. This phrase is ambiguous, perhaps intentionally. Although Aristotle speaks of the analogy between the claws of animals and the nails of men, I am unable to find any passage in which he suggests that the latter evolved out of the former. See *Parts of Animals*, 687ᵇ23-

25 and 690ᵇ8-11 (IV, x), (A. L. Peck, trans. [Loeb Classical Library; Cambridge: Harvard University Press, 1937], pp. 375, 391); and *History of Animals*, 486ᵇ20 (I, i), 502ᵇ1-5 (II, viii), and 517ª30-ᵇ1 (III, ix), (D'Arcy Wentworth Thompson, trans. [Oxford: Clarendon Press, 1910]). Even a cursory reading of these works reveals the gulf between Aristotle's biological method, which assumes that each species is naturally distinct, and the radically evolutionary approach of Rousseau. For example, Aristotle asserts that man stands erect on two feet because "his nature and essence is divine" (*Parts of Animals*, 686ª27-30 [IV, x]); nature forms each species in terms of its end or perfection. For Rousseau, it is distinctly possible that the human species has evolved from a stage in which man was a quadruped, and this hypothesis can only be rejected after the kind of physiological and biological analysis outlined in his note (*c*).

22. "So that in the first place, I put for a general inclination of all mankind, a perpetual and restless desire for power after power, that ceaseth only in death." Hobbes, *Leviathan*, I, xi. Compare *ibid.*, I, xiii-xiv.

23. See Montesquieu, *The Spirit of the Laws*, I, ii. Compare Pufendorf, *Le Droit de la Nature et des Gens*, II, i, § 8 and II, ii, § 2, as well as II, iii, § 16, where Barbeyrac quotes Cumberland (ed. 1706, I, 135, 137, and 182, n. 2). See also Richard Cumberland, *De Legibus Naturæ*, ii, § 29 (London: Nathanael Hooke, 1672), pp. 155-57.

24. See *Republic* III.405d ff, and compare Homer, *Iliad* XI. 639-40.

25. Compare Aristotle's view that "tame animals have a better nature than wild." *Politics* 1254ᵇ10 (I, ii).

26. Rousseau here cites Montaigne's "Of the Inequality Among Us" (*Essays*, I, xlii): "Plutarch says somewhere that he does not find so great a difference between one beast and another as he does between one man and an-

other . . . I shall gladly improve on Plutarch, and say that there is more difference between a given man and another than between a given man and a given beast." For another translation, see Zeitlin, I, 226. Montaigne's reference is to Plutarch's "That Beasts Use Reason," an essay cited by Rousseau in the *Social Contract*, I, ii.

27. Here Rousseau compares the development of the arts in Sparta (which was on the banks of the Eurotas river) and Athens. Compare *First Discourse*, p. 43.

28. Rousseau here alludes to the *Académie française*, which perpetually revises its Dictionary of the French language. Compare this slighting reference to the academies with the *First Discourse*, p. 59.

29. Note that, in this paragraph, Rousseau implies that Hobbes has established the correct definition of natural right. but that he has reasoned improperly concerning the implications of this definition. Compare the Preface of this *Discourse* (p. 94).

30. "To such an extent has ignorance of vices been more profitable to them [the Scythians] than the understanding of virtue to these [the Greeks]." Justin, *Histories*, II, ii. Although Rousseau is here silent about the context of the quotation, compare *First Discourse*, pp. 41-42, 51 with Justin's praise of the Scythians in Book II of his *Histories*. Compare Grotius, *Le Droit de la Guerre et de la Paix*, II, ii, § 2 (ed. 1724, p. 224).

31. The French term, here and throughout translated as "vanity," is *amour-propre*. *L'Amour de soi-même*, which Rousseau distinguishes sharply from *amour-propre*, will be translated as "love of oneself." Compare the use of the term *amour-propre* in Barbeyrac's translation of Pufendorf, *Le Droit de la Nature et des Gens*, II, iii, esp. § 14 and 16 (ed. 1706, I, 176-77, 183).

32. As the sequel shows, this "detractor" is Bernard Mandeville, whose *Fable of the Bees: or, Private Vices, Public Benefits* (1714) attempts to show that every virtue

is fundamentally based upon selfishness and private vice. In that work Mandeville says, speaking of charity: "This virtue is often counterfeited by a Passion of ours, call'd *Pity* or *Compassion*, which consists in a Fellow-feeling and Condolence for the Misfortunes and Calamities of others: all Mankind are more or less affected with it; but the weakest minds generally the most." See F. B. Kaye, ed., *The Fable of the Bees* (Oxford: Clarendon Press, 1924), p. 287.

33. This example from *The Fable of the Bees* is followed by the comment: "There would be no need of Virtue or Self-Denial to be moved at such a Scene; and not only a man of humanity, of good Morals and Commiseration, but likewise an Highwayman, an House-Breaker, or a Murderer could feel Anxieties on such an occasion." *Ibid.*, pp. 288-89. Mandeville's point is that pity is not truly a *virtue*, which he defines as "every Performance by which Man, contrary to the impulse of Nature, should endeavor the Benefit of others, or the Conquest of his own Passions out of a Rational Ambition of being good." *Ibid.*, p. 34. Despite his apparent attack on Mandeville, Rousseau agrees that pity is not a virtue in this sense; as is clear in the sequel, Rousseau considers pity to be a prerational impulse which does not override man's natural inclination to preserve himself should the two basic natural principles conflict. Compare Preface, *Second Discourse* (pp. 95-96), noting the qualification on the operation of natural pity.

34. Lucius Cornelius Sulla or Sylla (138-78 B.C.), a Roman general and politician who, having been victorious in a civil war, became the dictator of Rome. From this position he proscribed and killed many of those who were opposed to him. See Plutarch's *Lives*, "Sulla," II, VI, xxx-xxxi (Bernadotte Perrin, trans. [Loeb Classical Library; Cambridge: Harvard University Press, 1916], IV, 327-29, 341-43, 423-29).

35. Compare Montaigne's reference to the story in

"Cowardice the Mother of Cruelty" (*Essays*, II, xxvii):
"Alexander, Tyrant of Pherae, could not bear to listen to
tragedies presented at the theater for fear that his citizens
would see him moan at the misfortunes of Hecuba and
Andromache—he who, without pity, had so many people
cruelly murdered daily." In Zeitlin's edition, the passage
is at II, 348. The basic source is Plutarch's *Lives*, "Pelo-
pidas" XXIX (Bernadotte Perrin, trans. [Loeb Classical
Library; Cambridge: Harvard University Press, 1917], V,
413-15).

36. Translated freely: "Nature, who gave men tears,
confesses she gives the human race most tender hearts."
Juvenal, *Satires* XV. 131-33. This satire tells of the rivalry
of the "Ombites" and the "Tentyrites" in Egypt. Religious
differences and unbounded hatred lead the Tentyrites to
eat their enemies for sheer pleasure. Juvenal then describes
some extraordinarily violent deeds that did not lead to
cannibalism for the sake of mere enjoyment; on the basis
of these examples he concludes that pity is natural to man.

37. Locke, *Essay Concerning Human Understanding*,
IV, iii, § 18; Rousseau uses the translation of Pierre Coste,
which appeared under the title *Essai Philosophique Con-
cernant l'Entendement Humain* (Revised ed.; Amsterdam:
Henri Schelte, 1723), p. 698. Locke's "axiom" is also cited
by Barbeyrac in his Translator's Preface to Pufendorf's
Le Droit de la Nature et des Gens, § 2. (ed. 1706, I, v).
While the French translation of Locke reads: "Il ne
sauroit y avoir *de l'injustice* où il n'y a point de propriété,"
Rousseau inserts "*d'injure*" where the translation, following
the original, says "*de l'injustice*." Compare Hobbes,
Leviathan, I, xv. Rousseau's citation of Locke has an element of irony because, to this point in Rousseau's argument, there exists only "a sort of property"—i.e., mere
possession without any legal sanction. The origin of
property in the complete sense of the word does not occur,
according to Rousseau, until the division of labor has led

men to the brink of civil society. Compare pp. 139 and 146 with pp. 151 and 154.

38. Compare Lucretius, *De Rerum Natura* V. 1113-1135; 1241-1296. As has often been noted, Lucretius' poem, expounding Epicurean philosophy, served as a model for Rousseau's *Second Discourse*. On the civilizing role of gold and silver, see also Locke, *Second Treatise*, chap. v, esp. § 50.

39. See Grotius, *Le Droit de la Guerre et de la Paix*, II, ii, § 2. (ed. 1724, p. 228). Pufendorf gives a different interpretation of this formula, *Le Droit de la Nature et des Gens*, IV, iv, § 13 (ed. 1706, I, 463). Compare Rousseau's presentation of a "labor theory of value" as the basis of all property rights with Locke's *Second Treatise*, chap. v. Note also that a goddess is the source of laws whose purpose is the protection of property, and that these laws create a "new kind of right"; it appears that gods are introduced by men to sanctify private property (which would otherwise be insecure). Compare Lucretius, *De Rerum Natura*, V. 1136-1240.

40. Compare the second sentence of the *Social Contract*, I, i: "One who thinks himself the master of others does not fail to be more of a slave than they."

41. "Shocked by the newness of the ill, rich and yet wretched, he seeks to run away from his wealth and hates what he once prayed for." Ovid, *Metamorphoses* XI. 127-28. The quotation describes the condition of Midas after Bacchus has granted his wish that everything he touch turn to gold.

42. Compare this passage with the apparent criticism of philosophers for their isolation from the common people (p. 132).

43. Since Rousseau has just discussed one form of this "supposition"—i.e., the argument that societies are formed by conquest—the remark is ironic.

44. See Pliny the Younger, *Panegyricus* LV, 7.

45. Compare note (*p*), pp. 223-24.

46. "The most wretched servitude they call peace." In Tacitus, *Histories* IV, xvii, the efforts of Civilis to incite the Gauls to revolt against Rome are described; Civilis "warned them in secret speeches of those evils they had suffered for so many years, while a wretched servitude they falsely called peace (*miseram servitutem falso pacem vocarent*)." Rousseau's citation of this phrase follows the version of Algernon Sidney, *Discourses Concerning Government*, chap. ii, § 15 (London: Booksellers of London and Westminster, 1698), p. 125.

47. See Locke, *First Treatise*, chaps. ii, vi, vii, ix, and *Second Treatise*, chap. vi; and Sidney, *Discourses Concerning Government*, chap. i, § 6-20; chap. ii, § 2-4; and chap. iii, § 1.

48. The work in question is the *Traité des Droits de la Reine très Chrétienne sur divers États de la Monarchie d'Espagne*, an attempt to justify Louis XIV's dubious claims to certain Spanish possessions—claims which served as the basis of the War of Devolution (1667-68). By referring to an example of the Sun King's flagrantly expansionist policy, Rousseau again "damns with false praise" (compare *First Discourse*, editorial note 49). Lest this interpretation of Rousseau's quotation be thought tendentious, Sidney used this passage of the *Traité des Droits de la Reine* to criticize absolute monarchy; see *Discourses Concerning Government*, chap. ii, § 30 (ed. 1698, p. 235). Barbeyrac also pointed out the irony of this profession of limited authority by Louis XIV in his translation of Pufendorf, *Le Droit de la Nature et des Gens*, VII, vi, § 10, n.1 (ed. 1706, II, 273).

49. *Ibid.*, VII, viii, § 6, n. 2 (ed. 1706, II, 302). For the original, see Locke, *Second Treatise*, chap, iv, § 23. It is not an accident that, instead of quoting Locke directly, Rousseau cites (and is willing to neglect) the "authority of Barbeyrac"; compare Rousseau's remarks on the authoritative character of Barbeyrac in the *Social Contract*, II, ii.

50. Pufendorf, *Le Droit de la Nature et des Gens*, VII, iii, §1 and vi, §5 (ed. 1706, II, 223, 265-66). Cf. Grotius, *Le Droit de la Guerre et de la Paix*, I, iii, §8 (ed. 1724, pp. 121-24).

51. Note the tentative character of Rousseau's remarks concerning the social contract, and compare the "common opinion" to which he here restricts himself with the formulations of Hobbes's *Leviathan*, II, xvii-xviii, and Locke's *Second Treatise*, chaps. viii (esp. § 95-98) and xix. Rousseau implicitly distinguishes the "fundamental compact of all governments" from the original bond of a society without a government—those "general conventions which all individuals pledged to observe, and regarding which the community became the guarantor for each individual" (p. 163). Compare the "common opinion" which Rousseau claims he is "following" with the "supposition which does not permit of serious debate" (*ibid.*).

52. Compare this preliminary discussion of the relationship between the magistrates and the laws produced by the "single will" of the people with the concept of the "general will" and the subordination of the "government" to the "sovereign" in the *Social Contract*, esp. I, vi-vii; II, i-vi; and III, i.

53. Note the implication that religion has served to protect illegitimate government from overthrow, and compare Rousseau's remarks on religion in the *Social Contract*, esp. II, vii and IV, viii.

54. The French word *seigneur* is derived from the Latin word *senior*, the comparative of *senex* (old); "the authority accorded to age made the meaning of old man shift to that of *seigneur*." E. Littré, *Dictionnaire de la Langue Française* (Paris: Hachette, 1869), II-ii, 1953.

55. Compare V. I. Lenin, *Imperialism*, esp. chaps. viii and x.

56. "If it is in my brother's breast that you order me to sink my sword, or in my father's throat, or even in the unborn child in my pregnant wife's womb, I shall do it all,

even if my right hand is unwilling." Lucan, *Pharsalia* I. 376-78. In this passage, Laelius is answering Caesar's cry to march on Rome, and in so doing overcomes the doubts of the soldiers. As Vaughan points out (I, 193, n. 3), Rousseau substitutes *gravidæque* for *plenæque;* the same substitution will be found in the citation of this passage by Sidney, *Discourses Concerning Government,* chap. ii, § 19 (ed. 1698, p. 147).

57. "In which there is no hope to be derived from an honorable deed," a variant of a phrase in Tacitus (*pauci, quis nulla ex honesto spes*), *Annals* V, iii. Compare Sidney, *Discourses Concerning Government,* chap. ii, § 20, where the phrase *quibus ex honesto nulla est spes* is used (ed. 1698, p. 150).

58. Compare Montaigne, "Of Cannibals," *Essays,* I, xxxi (Zeitlin, I, 190).

59. See Herodotus, *Histories,* III, 83. "Then Otanes, his proposal to give the Persians equality being defeated, thus spoke among them all: 'Friends and partisans! Seeing that it is plain that one of us must be made king (whether by lot, or by our suffering the people of Persia to choose whom they will, or in some other way), know that I will not enter the lists with you; I desire neither to rule nor to be ruled; but if I waive my claim to be king, I make this condition, that neither I nor any of my posterity shall be subject to any one of you.' To these terms the six others agreed; Otanes took no part in the contest but stood aside; and to this day his house (and none other in Persia) remains free, nor is compelled to render any unwilling obedience, so long as it transgresses no Persian law." A. D. Godley, trans. (Loeb Classical Library; Cambridge: Harvard University Press, 1938), II, iii.

60. Note that Rousseau here assumes that it is logically necessary for the binding power of law to be general. Compare *Social Contract,* esp. I, vi and II, iv. Hence this remark also implies the distinction between the laws, which

are enacted by the Sovereign, and decrees or other applications of the law by the Government or Prince (see *ibid.*, II, v; and III, i).

61. Compare Herodotus, *Histories*, III, 141, 147, 149.

62. This passage from Buffon's *Histoire Naturelle, De la nature de l'homme*, implies the validity of modern natural science as an "authority" for philosophy, at least insofar as its reasoning is "solid and sublime." Note the character of Rousseau's remaining notes. Rousseau refers to the edition of the *Histoire Naturelle, Générale et Particulière* in 12° (Paris: Imprimerie Royale, 1752, reprinted in 1774), IV, 151-152. Vaughan also makes reference to the edition in 4° (Paris: Imprimerie Royale, 1749, second edition 1750), II, 429-30.

63. Étienne Bonnot de Condillac, *Essai sur l'Origine des Connoissances Humaines*, I, iv, chap. ii, § 23 (2 vols.; Amsterdam: Pierre Mortier, 1746), I, 202-3.

64. Note the radical character of Rousseau's analysis of man's natural condition and his use of empirical examples of humans born outside of society (i.e., in a "true" state of nature). Compare editorial note 21 to the *Second Discourse*.

65. The Northwest Division of Arabia (extending along the Red Sea from the Gulf of Akabah to about the parallel of 20 North Latitude, and including Mecca and Medina).

66. Buffon, *Histoire Naturelle, Générale et Particulière, Preuves de la théorie de la terre*, art. 7 (2nd ed. in 4°, 1750), I, 242-43.

67. A Fourth Century disciple of Aristotle known as a historian and geographer; few fragments of his works are extant.

68. St. Jerome, *Against Jovinianus*, II, § 13. Rousseau omits the equation, in the original, of the reign of Saturn with the Golden Age. See Philip Schaff and Henry Wace, eds., *A Select Library of Nicene and Post-Nicene Fathers of the Christian Church*, Second Series (New York: Chris-

tian Literature Co., 1893), VI, 397. This sentence was cited by Barbeyrac in his translation of Grotius, *Le Droit de la Guerre et de la Paix*, II, ii, § 2, n. 13 (ed. 1724, p. 225). Compare the two discourses "On Eating Meat" in Plutarch's *Moralia*.

69. Compare note (*j*) pp. 207-13.

70. Antoine François Prévost, ed., *Histoire Générale des Voyages* (20 vols.; Paris: Didot, 1746-91), V, 157. The first seven volumes of this compendium were a translation of John Green's *A New General Collection of Voyages and Travels* (London: T. Astley, 1745-47). The passage quoted here is a paraphrase of Peter Kolben (or Pierre Kolbe), *Description du Cap de Bonne-Espérance*, I, xxiii, § 7-8 (3 vols.; Amsterdam: Jean Catuffe, 1742), I, 396-99. According to the sources, the Hottentots swim with their *neck* (*col*) upright, not their *body* (*corps*).

71. *Histoire Générale des Voyages*, V, 155-56. In both quotations from this work, Rousseau omits remarks which are not relevant to his point. The original source is Kolben, *Description du Cap de Bonne-Espérance*, I, vi, § 14 (I, 99-100) and I, xi, § 10 (I, 195-97).

72. The work in question is *Observations sur l'Histoire Naturelle, sur la Physique, et sur la Peinture*, a periodical first published in Paris in 1752 under the editorship of Jacques Gautier d'Agoty.

73. Buffon, *Histoire Naturelle, Générale et Particulière, Histoire naturelle du cheval* (2nd Ed. in 4°, 1750), IV, 226-27.

74. On this entire note, compare Rousseau's Letter to Voltaire, 18 August 1756, *Correspondance Générale*, II, 303-9. In this letter Rousseau also argues that all nature follows regular laws, which could conceivably be understood by means of modern science (*ibid.*, pp. 309-14).

75. See Montaigne, "The Profit of One Man is the Damage of Another," *Essays*, I, xxii (Zeitlin, I, 91).

76. See Rousseau's *L'état de guerre* (Vaughan, I, 302-3).

77. Compare Montesquieu, *Persian Letters*, cxii-cxxii, and *Spirit of the Laws*, XXIII, esp. xv-xxviii.

78. I.e., those who claim descent from a divinely inspired ancestor like Abraham—hence, most particularly, those believing in the Judeo-Christian (and Moslem) religions.

79. This obscure phrase implies that for some men religion is respectable only because it serves the necessary social function of making conventional morality appear to be divinely ordained (and not because man's first ancestor was, like Adam in the Garden of Eden, truly moral). Compare Machiavelli, *Discourses on Titus Livy*, I, xi.

80. This long note summarizes some of the main themes of the *First Discourse*, to which it should be compared. Rousseau's denial that he intends to lead men back into the forests should be emphasized; the state of nature provides a standard for judging civil society, but not a practical and generally applicable prescription for reform.

81. *Histoire Générale des Voyages*, V, 87-89.

82. With great delicacy, Rousseau here proposes the experimental cross-breeding of orangutans and humans as a possible proof of the status of the former as men in the pure state of nature. Rousseau thereby suggests one possible solution to the task ascribed to the "Aristotles and Plinys of our century" in the Preface to the *Second Discourse* (above, p. 93).

83. Compare Aristotle's *Politics* 1253^{a}3-5 (I, ii): "He who is without a polis, by reason of his own nature and not of some accident, is either a poor sort of being, or a being higher than man . . ." Ernest Barker, trans. (Oxford: Clarendon Press, 1946), p. 5.

84. See the passage of Condillac's *Essai sur l'Origine des Connoissances Humaines* cited above, note 63.

85. This long note indicates clearly the extent to which modern anthropology and the comparative study of cultures and politics may be said to derive from the theoretical position set forth by Rousseau.

86. In the following passage, Rousseau transcribes an anonymous French translation of Locke's *Second Treatise*, chap. vii, § 79-80. Here Locke's English is quoted, following the second edition (London: Awnsham and John Churchill, 1694), pp. 224-25. Where the original differs from the French translation used by Rousseau, the latter is followed.

87. This distinction between the natural process of a child's development and existing patterns of education in society is obviously the root of Rousseau's conception of a natural education as it is developed in *Émile*.

88. This long note, with its criticism of Locke, and the text to which it is appended clearly deny the natural status of the human family. Rousseau elsewhere took a less extreme view, more closely parallel to Locke's. "The most ancient of all societies, and the only natural one, is that of the family. Even so, the children only remain bound to their father for as long as they have need of him for their self-preservation. As soon as this need ceases, the natural bond is dissolved. The children exempt from the obedience they owed their father, the father exempt from the cares he owed his children, all return equally to independence. If they continue to remain united, it is no longer naturally, but voluntarily; and the family itself is only maintained by convention." *Social Contract*, I, ii. Compare also *Émile*, v (Hachette, II, 401), where Rousseau implies that there may be a "kind of marriage' by nature.

89. "Nor would anything of the happiness of the human race disappear if, when the crowd and confusion of so many languages has been expelled, [all] mortals should cultivate [this] one art and if it should be permitted to explain anything with signs, movements, and actions. But now it has so been established that the condition of animals that are popularly believed to be brutes is far better than ours in this regard, inasmuch as they indicate their feelings and thoughts without an interpreter more readily and

perhaps more happily than any mortals can, especially if they use a foreign language." Isaac Vossius, *De Poematum Cantu et Viribus Rythmi* (Oxford: Theatro Sheldoniano, 1673), pp. 65-66. The words in brackets are omitted in Rousseau's quotation of the original.

90. Plato, *Republic*, VII. 522. Plato's discussion of the relationship between the science of numbers and philosophic speculation is highly relevant to Rousseau's argument in this note.

91. Reproduced p. 76.

92. The original source of the story is Kolben, *Description du Cap de Bonne-Espérance*, I, xii, § 11 (ed. 1742, I, 234-35).

93. Isocrates, *Areopagitica*, 21-22. See George Norlin, trans., *Isocrates* (Loeb Classical Library; London: William Heinemann, 1929), II, 117.

94. This note is of particular importance. On the one hand, Rousseau criticizes Hobbes's rejection of the classical conception of "distributive justice," while on the other he seeks to limit the role of law to the establishment of perfectly general and impersonal standards. The classical view that all regimes are based on a principle of distributive justice—i.e., a principle of rewarding personal merit by "distinguishing and favoring" individuals in proportion to their intrinsic worth—is set forth most clearly in Book V of Aristotle's *Ethics*, 1130^b30-1131^b24. Aristotle distinguishes between such "distributive justice," in which awards are made "according to merit," and "commutative" or "rectificatory justice": the latter treats all men as equal and merely attempts to correct or punish specific actions regardless of the personal merits of the individuals in question. In Chapter xv of the *Leviathan*, Hobbes explicitly criticizes the classical distinction, arguing that the reward for merit "is not due by justice; but is rewarded of grace only"—i.e., the only relevant standard in political life is commutative justice, which treats every subject of

the laws equally regardless of his personal worth. Rousseau, after quoting from Isocrates, asserts that standards of distributive justice are necessarily present in all societies, however corrupt, but he diverges sharply from the classical view by limiting the scope of legal provisions to *actions*. The resulting distinction between "morals" and "right" or "law," which characterizes modern thought generally, presupposes that laws can never be used as the basis of rewards for personal virtue. Whereas other modern political philosophers tended to reject the classical standard of virtue (thereby rejecting distributive justice in favor of commutative justice as the basis of the political order), Rousseau attempted to use modern principles in order to found a political society in which the classical notion of virtue might still have a place. Compare *Social Contract*, IV, vii.